Debt Forgiveness, Volume 2
When Creditors Decide to Sue
---Second Edition---

Arthur V. Prosper

Copyright©2016 by Arthur V. Prosper * A-Team Publishing Group * PO Box 153 * Pinebrook, New Jersey 07058

COPYRIGHT AND TRADEMARK OWNERSHIP

All rights reserved. No part of this publication may be reproduced, stored in a retrieval system or transmitted by any means, electronic, mechanical, photocopying, recording, scanning or otherwise except as permitted under Section 107 or 108 of the 1976 United States Copyright Act, without the prior permission of the author and publisher. Please be aware that any unauthorized use of the contents contained herein violates copyright laws, trademark laws, the laws of privacy and publicity, and/or other regulations and statutes. All text, images and other materials provided herein are owned by **Arthur V. Prosper** unless otherwise attributed to third parties. None of the content on these materials may be copied, reproduced, distributed, downloaded, displayed, or transmitted in any form without the prior written permission of **Arthur V. Prosper**, the legal copyright owner. However, you may copy, reproduce, distribute, download, display, or transmit the content of the materials for personal, non-commercial use provided that full attribution and citation to **Arthur V. Prosper** is included and the content is not modified, and you retain all copyright and other proprietary notices contained in the content. The permission stated above is automatically rescinded if you breach any of these terms or conditions. If permission is rescinded or denied, you must immediately destroy any downloaded and/or printed content.

FBI Anti-Piracy Warning: The unauthorized reproduction or distribution of a copyrighted work is illegal. Criminal copyright infringement, including infringement without monetary gain, is investigated by the FBI and is punishable by up to five years in federal prison and a fine of $250,000.

PAPERBACK ISBN: 978-1976956973
Imprint: Independently published by:
A-Team, PO Box 153, Pinebrook, NJ 07058
Cover Design by: Kristjan Victorino
Printed in the United States
Author's Email Address: arthurvprosper@gmail.com

Also by Arthur V. Prosper

The Simplest Path to Wealth: Turn $50,000 into $3.3 Million

Stop Paying Your Credit Cards: Obtain Credit Card Debt Forgiveness Vol 1

Dynamic Budgeting Techniques: Cut your expenses in half and double your income

How Much Federal Income Tax Will I Pay in 2018? The New Tax Law's winners and losers

The Six Million Dollar Retiree: Your roadmap to a six million dollar retirement nest egg

Living Rich & Loving It: Your guide to a rich, happy, healthy, simple and balanced life

Copyright©2016 by Arthur V. Prosper

DISCLAIMER

Notice: The information contained in this book is provided to you "AS IS" and does not constitute legal advice. All sample forms are for educational purposes only. We make no claims, promises or guarantees about the accuracy, completeness, or any specific result from the use of the contents or adequacy of the information contained in this book. Information contained in this book should not be used as substitute for obtaining legal advice from an attorney licensed or authorized to practice in your jurisdiction. The author is not a lawyer. No warranties are made regarding the suitability of this book. This book contains an accumulation of information based on the personal experience of the author. Prior results do not guarantee a similar outcome.

All rights reserved. No part of this book may be reproduced by any means without prior permission from the author.

****

If you have questions or comments, visit the author's website at: http://Arthur V. Prosper.com/

****

Copyright©2016 by Arthur V. Prosper

Contents

- About the Author 6
- Preface to the Second Edition 9
- Introduction 10
- Take My Offer or Sue Me 13
- Review the timeline 15
- Negotiation-Resistant Creditors 19
- Junk Debt Collectors Try to Collect on Old Judgments 23
- Why Creditors Prefer to Sue 25
- Validation of Debt, Cease and Desist Letter - Sample 30
- When Creditor Ignores Validation of Debt Letter 33
- Creditors May Sue in Court or File for an Arbitration Hearing 36
- Refusal of Arbitration 38
- Creditor/Plaintiff's Complaint 41
- Sample Answer to Complaint 43
- More Sample Complaints and Answers 50
- Request for Production of Documents 53
- Creditor/Plaintiff's Motion for Summary Judgment 59
- Collections attorney claims he is not a "debt collector" ... 69
- Do you have to pay tax on the cancelled debt? 72
- How to Mitigate Negative Credit Report 75
- 5 Smart Ways to Improve Your Credit 80
- Factors That Affect Credit Scores 81
- The bank can freeze your checking and savings accounts 87
- What really happens after creditor files suit? 88
- Conclusion – Volume 2 99
- The Simplest Path to Wealth: Turn $50,000 into $3.3 Million 101

Living Rich and Loving It: 102

More ABOUT THE AUTHOR 106

Supplemental Disclaimer 106

Copyright and Trademark Ownership 107

About the Author

Arthur V. Prosper is a freelance writer, author and columnist with 30 years of market experience. He writes articles about the markets, business, finance and politics under the header "DidoSphere, DidoSpin and Vox Populi". He is the author of several published articles including: How We Got Here, Market Crash of 2008, Housing Bubble, The Obama Recession, Bank Stress Tests & Other Terms, Scrap Mark to Market Valuation, Recession Over, The Labyrinth of Obamacare, Bush-Obama Recession, No Different From the Rest, A Tale of Two States, NJ & VA, SEC's Case vs. GS&CO., Weak, Most Experts Agree, PIIGS: Too Big to Fail, What Causes Stock Market Fluctuations, Sluggish Recovery, Good for Investors, QE2=Printing Money, Stock Market Investors, Fasten Your Seatbelt, No Double Dip Recession, 10% Unemployment Rate, Not Enough to Derail Recovery
****

If you need advice on budgeting, personal money management, investing, funding college education and retirement planning, download the author's new cradle to grave, guide-to-life book, *"Living Rich and Loving It"*,

https://www.amazon.com/Living-Rich-Loving-healthy-balanced-ebook/dp/B01GORIB4Y/ref=sr_1_3?s=digital-text&ie=UTF8&qid=1465482641&sr=1-3&keywords=Arthur V. Prosper

- You will learn how to:
  - Create a simple budget so you will always have a surplus at month end
  - Maximize contributions to your retirement account
  - Never lose money in the stock market
  - Predict the start and the end of a recession
  - Buy your principal residence
  - Choose between a traditional 401k and a Roth 401k
  - Accumulate over $3 million in your retirement account
  - Calculate the amount of life insurance you need
  - Determine the right time to start collecting social security
  - Maximize your Social Security benefits
  - Pay for long-term care
  - Qualify for Medicaid
  - Preserve your lifetime savings
  - Manage emergencies without "an emergency fund"
  - Find the job you love
  - Fund your children's college education
  - Find creative ways to increase your income
  - Create a document storage and retrieval system
  - Implement a personal time management system
  - Store and safeguard passwords
  - Plan for retirement
  - Locate the best places to retire

- Spend your leisure time wisely
- Stay healthy and fit
- Live a rich, happy and healthy life

****

Preface to the Second Edition

This is the Second Edition of the book, ***Debt Forgiveness, Volume 2 – When Creditors Decide to Sue"***. This Second Edition was published on July 15, 2018.

The First Edition, published on January 8, 2016, covered various scenarios as to what might happen if a creditor refuses to negotiate a reduction or complete forgiveness of your alleged debt and takes the legal route instead, putting your account immediately into litigation. Strategies and methods were discussed in the First Edition; necessary updates were incorporated into this Second Edition. Moreover, new information as to the behavior of creditors, collectors and attorneys, derived from readers' experiences, as reported by readers, have been added to this Second Edition.

Introduction

I want to thank you for purchasing the book, ***"Debt Forgiveness, Volume 2 – When Creditors Decide to Sue"***. If this book helped you, your positive review would be much appreciated.

What this book IS about:

      This book will guide the reader on what to do if the creditor/collector decides to file a Civil Complaint. Yes you can answer a law suit on your own as a Pro-se Defendant (representing yourself without legal counsel) AND WIN but there are many traps, land mines and pitfalls that a do-it-yourselfer can fall into that may end up costing you more money than the original amount claimed by your creditor if you fail to follow the correct steps. A creditor/collector will file suit not because they want to drag you in front of a judge for a full blown trial. A trial is very expensive for a Plaintiff (creditor/collector) and their chance of winning is not good. In the 1998 movie, "A CIVIL ACTION", Jan Schlichtmann played by John Travolta said:

"The odds of a plaintiff's lawyer winning in civil court are two to one against. Think about that for a second. Your (the plaintiff) odds of surviving a game of Russian roulette are better than winning a case at trial. 12 times better. So why does anyone do it? They don't. They settle. Out of the 780,000, only 12,000 or 1 1/2 percent ever reach a verdict. The whole idea of lawsuits is to settle, to compel the other side to settle. And you do that by spending more money than you should, which forces them to spend more money than they should, and whoever comes to their senses first loses. Trials are a corruption of the entire process and only fools who have something to prove end up ensnared in them".

Creditors/Collectors file suits because, 1) if you do not answer the suit, they can win a default judgment against you after which they may be able to garnish your wages, freeze your bank accounts and/or put a lien on your properties, 2) to scare you into paying the full amount of the claim, 3) to force you into negotiation. Now that you know the Plaintiffs' objectives when they file Complaints, your objective should be to convince the Plaintiff that you are prepared to go to trial…even if you are not and do not really want to. This book will help you accomplish this goal.

We learned in Volume 1 that you can obtain credit card debt forgiveness if you write your creditors a simple, properly worded negotiation letter. This book, Volume 2 in this series is about various measures you can take if your creditors refuse to cooperate and decide to sue instead. The methods and strategies in this book may be put to use in dealing with credit card debt as well as other unsecured loans and consumer debt such as payday loans, doctors' and hospital bills, department stores and furniture stores and home improvement loans that you cannot afford to pay anymore. This book contains sample forms such as, Request for Validation of Debt, Cease and Desist, Plaintiff's Complaint, Answer and Affirmative Defenses to Plaintiff's Complaint, Request for Production of Documents, Refusal of Arbitration, Opposition to Plaintiff's Motion for Summary Judgment, Defendant's Motion for Summary Judgment, sample letter to IRS disputing creditor's 1099-C (CODI-Cancellation of Debt Income).

Volume 1 provided the reader with the means for negotiating credit card debt down to 5% and gave the reader a better understanding of the actions and reactions of the creditors, collectors and attorneys involved in the collection process. This volume provides the necessary tools to deal with the negotiation-resistant creditor and to use the system legally to obtain debt cancellation. This book contains a wealth of information derived from many hours of research and through trial and error.

Although there are no guarantees, the methods and strategies discussed in this book worked for me. When I sent my creditors a Request for Validation of Debts shown in this book, my creditors were not able to validate my alleged debts. My creditors could not produce the documents requested on my Request for Production of Documents. The Court denied the Plaintiff's Motion for Summary Judgment when I filed my Opposition to the Motion. When I answered the creditors' law suits (see my Answer to Complaint under Chapter, "Creditor/Plaintiff's Complaint"), they abandoned the case and never showed up in Court. When I disputed the creditors' Forms 1099-C and requested the IRS to obtain verification of debt from the creditors pursuant to U.S. Code – Title 26 Section 6201(d), I never heard from the IRS again.

After my debts were forgiven, the nightmare was over so I was able to start my life anew, free from credit card debt. I was able to focus on taking care of my family. I kept 2 credit cards and continued to use them. They carried small credit limits, one for $7,000 and the other for $5,000. The credit limits have since increased to $15,000 each. Now I pay the balances of the accounts as soon as I receive the monthly statements. The credit card companies reported the amounts to reporting agencies as "Charge Off", so my FICO credit scores initially took a dive to the high 500s. When I contested the "Charge Off" amounts and insisted that the creditors report them as "paid as agreed", my FICO scores started climbing gradually. After only 7 years, I am back to the high 700s and even got to 800 for a few months last year. Only a few years after my debts were forgiven, I started receiving pre-approved credit card offers in the mail again. But I have not applied for any new credit cards. I feel really blessed that I did not have to file for bankruptcy and that the path I took enabled me to write this book which I hope will help a lot of people, who are in the same predicament I was, and to accomplish the same thing I've accomplished---a credit card debt free life.

Take My Offer or Sue Me

If you google "Stop paying your credit card debt" or "credit card debt settlement negotiation" you will find many articles and books offering expert advice on how to negotiate credit card debt forgiveness. If you believe what they say, you will notice that many of the authors of these books usually succeed in negotiating about 50% reduction of the debt which to the authors seems like a great accomplishment. Somehow a 50% debt reduction makes them a "guru" on the subject. I suppose if you owe $100,000 of credit card debt and received a discount of $50,000, you may think "I'm on the top of the world". I am not greedy, but I negotiated to pay only 10% of what I owed because at that time that was all I could afford to pay as a cash settlement and my creditors were happy to accept it. Well, at least they did not say otherwise. I had to take the hardline with my creditors, tough it out and look out for myself and my family. It was pretty much "take my settlement offer or sue me". But if you do, you will lose. I am very suspicious of positive reviewers of some of these books dealing with debt settlement and debt negotiation. Some of them make fantastic claims such as, "This book helped me settle my $50,000 balance for $10,000". It is not that easy. Unless you follow the step by step procedures in Volume 1 of this series, chances are the credit card companies will sue you first and try to win a $50,000 judgment against you instead of agreeing to an 80% discount. It is easy enough for them to do this and definitely cheaper than accepting 20% as full settlement of your debt particularly if they think you have some assets they can attach or income they can garnish. See the chapter, "What will the creditors do when you stop paying" in Volume 1 of this series,
https://www.amazon.com/Stop-Paying-Your-Credit-Cards-ebook/dp/B019ZY3D1E/ref=asap_bc?ie=UTF8

which discusses the filing of Complaints in bulk by creditors' attorneys. As soon as you receive a summons from your creditor for a Complaint demanding $50,000 plus legal fees, the odds shift in their favor. How will you answer the Complaint? What is your excuse (defense) for not paying your $50,000 debt? That is why *The Letter* in Volume 1 is so important and serves as your first line of defense. The wording of *The Letter* conveys to your creditors that you have the skill, ability and inclination to answer, oppose and defeat their legal actions. If you show the creditors that they still will not collect more than your FINAL OFFER even if they file a lawsuit; that they will only spend a lot of money in legal fees, they will realize that collecting 10% from you is probably the best they can hope to recover. That is the aim of the negotiation letter shown in Volume 1, to show your creditors that your FINAL OFFER is the most they can collect from you. But if your creditors are stubborn and negotiation-resistant, this book Volume 2 is your magic bullet against them. If you decide NOT to purchase this book Volume 2, you won't know what to do without an expensive attorney if you get sued. You will be at the mercy of your creditors.

Review the timeline

The following is a sample timeline as to what may happen from the moment you stop paying your credit card completely if you do not follow my system:
- STOPPED PAYING YOUR CREDIT CARD ACCOUNT COMPLETELY.
- CC Company will send you a statement the following month with additional interests.
- CC Company will send you a statement a month later with added interests and possibly additional late fees.
- After 60 days, CC Company will send you a new statement with late fees and possibly additional interests computed at a higher rate (penalty interest) which can be as high as 30%. The CC's in house collector will keep calling you probably several times a day. The collector may even call you at your place of work.
- After 90 days, collection efforts usually intensify and the collector usually writes a letter or calls to inform you that your delinquency will be reported to credit reporting agencies. Collectors may also sound sympathetic and may give you the impression that they are willing to work with you by lowering your interest and your minimum payments. At this juncture, you may be tempted to accept their offer to pay a small amount out of fear especially since your balance keeps going up even though you have not been making additional purchases. It is psychological warfare at this point. You don't know the end game and your balance has probably increased by 12% since you first stopped paying. It will be a mistake to make even a very small payment because that can restart the collection clock and the collection attorney may use the resumption of payments as an admission of your debt.

- The intensified collection efforts will continue until the end of six months after your delinquency. At which time, the CC Company may choose to charge off your account so as to enable them to write off the debt as a bad debt which is a deductible expense on their corporate tax return. If they do this, they will report your debt as "charge off" to reporting agencies. They may refer your account to a local attorney for collection on a contingency basis or sell it outright to a junk debt collector for between 5 and 10% of the balance.
- The junk debt collector will restart the collection process and can make your life miserable. Some unscrupulous collectors may even violate a few FDCPA collection rules such as calling you before 8am and after 9pm, not disclosing that they are a debt collector, giving the impression that the collector is a lawyer and that you can be arrested if you do not pay your debt.
- A local attorney who may work for the CC Company for a fee or on contingency may initially send just the casual pre-printed collection letters. After 60 to 90 days, if you do not reply, he may send you a FINAL NOTICE BEFORE SUIT. This final notice is usually sent by certified mail to impress upon you that this has become a serious matter.
- If the attorney does not receive a reply, he may actually file suit and you will receive a summons together with the Complaint. See the Chapter, Creditor's/Plaintiff's Complaint. The Complaint will include the attorney's fees and court filing fees. You generally have 30 days to reply to the Complaint in most jurisdictions.
- If you do not reply to the Complaint, the attorney will file a motion for default judgment and the judge may grant him that judgment.
- In most states, the attorney may be allowed to file a Writ of Garnishment or Writ of Execution to collect on the

judgment and to direct your employer to garnish (deduct) a certain amount from your wages; the banks to turn over your money to satisfy the judgment; record a lien and seize or sell your properties through a sheriff's sale. In most states, your primary residence (homestead) is exempt from execution but other states have monetary limits on the homestead value that may be exempted from seizure.

If you follow my system, what is likely to happen is that the original creditor (cc Company), collector, collection attorney or junk debt collector will give up without a lawsuit. The letters in these books will convey the message that you have the time, skill and inclination to answer and oppose the creditor's Complaint and that it will not be profitable for the attorney and the original creditor to go through the expense of filing suit with worse than a 50/50 chance of winning. NO ONE really wants to go to court including attorneys. But in the unlikely event that they DO file a lawsuit against you, they will lose. You will answer the lawsuit, send them interrogatories and request production of documents. This is the step by step system: 1) Write *The Letter* (see The Letter in volume 1 – "Obtain Credit Card Debt Forgiveness", https://www.amazon.com/Stop-Paying-Your-Credit-Cards-ebook/dp/B019ZY3D1E/ref=asap_bc?ie=UTF8 2) stop making payments, 3) wait 30 days for a reply, 4) negotiate a lower amount if the creditor wants more than 15%, 5) write up with 2 or 3 follow up letters if the creditor is not replying or is refusing to come down to 15% or lower, 6) write a Validation of Debt, Cease and Desist Letter, 7) write letters to challenge CC Company's validation of debt (see these letters under Chapter "Validation of Debt, Cease and Desist"), 8) reply to the creditor's Complaint if you get sued, 9) mail the Plaintiff a Request for Production of Documents, Admissions and Interrogatories, 10) file a Motion for Summary Judgment.

If you do not follow the system, the creditor's attorney may be more inclined to file a lawsuit thinking that they will have an easy path in winning a default judgment against you if you have not followed my system of constant communication and sounding like a quasi-attorney. If they win a judgment against you, it will be a bigger nightmare for you. You may just hear the sheriff knocking at your door to seize your assets for a sheriff's sale. Our strategy here is not to let it get to the point where the creditor's attorney thinks that you will not fight a lawsuit. And that can be accomplished by conveying the message that you are willing and able to fight them in court and that they will be "spending more money than they should". Just like John Travolta's character said in the movie, "The whole idea of lawsuits is to settle, to compel the other side to settle". So no one ever wants to go to court for a trial.

Negotiation-Resistant Creditors

      Lately, creditors have wised-up and have been ignoring *"The Letter"*. Many of them are becoming more and more "negotiation-resistant". They simply reply with a form letter such as the one shown below:

****

Dear Credit Card Holder:
      This letter is in response to your correspondence received regarding your account. We understand that borrowers may experience income reductions, financial difficulties or life changes that can affect their ability to make payments, but informing our office of your current financial situation does not release you from your contractual obligation to pay in a timely manner. Please be assured that we want to work with you to determine an acceptable payment arrangement that works for all parties. Please contact Mary O. at (800) 555-1212, extension 69, or John T. at extension 96 to discuss options that may be available for the account.

Sincerely,
Credit Card Company

****

See Volume 1 of this series to find out how to respond to such a letter. You definitely MUST NOT call them. After 180 days, the likelihood is that the creditor will just mark your account "Charge Off", report your account to the 3 major credit reporting agencies as such and sell your account to a junk debt collector for 10% or less or refer your account to a local attorney. Why they would rather do this than settle with you for 10% is a complete mystery to me. They must have some type of a protocol, a procedure they follow. Or maybe they found out in the past that they will spend more time settling with you for 10% than simply handing your account over to a junk debt collector for 10%. But this is when the miserable collection process starts anew which gives you a new opportunity to negotiate with a junk debt collector for 15% of the total or lower. If they accept your payment as full and final settlement of your account, make sure the **collector and the original creditor** sign the "release". A sample release form is shown in Volume 1. If the creditor refers your account to a local attorney, one would think that they have the upper hand, but don't despair. Lawyers' stock in trade is their time. They will bail out from your case if the amount they think they can collect from you is not worth their time. They will initially send the debtor several standard collection letters like the original creditor did the moment you missed your minimum payment, followed by a "Final Notice before the filing of a suit". It is important to respond immediately to every attorney's collection letter to drive the point that you know what you are doing and that this case won't be an easy one for the attorney. As soon as I receive the first collection letter from an attorney, I write the following:

****

Certified Mail
Date: xx/xx/xx
RE: Account No. ########, Original Creditor Xxxxx
Dear Attorney Xxxxxxx:

  I am in receipt of your collection letter dated xx/xx/xx regarding the above referenced account. Please be informed that this alleged debt is unverified. I requested a "Validation of Debt" in accordance with the Fair Debt Collection Practices Act, 15 USC 1692g Sec. 809 (b), that your client's claim is disputed and validation is requested. See attached copy of my Validation of Debt request and a copy of the green postal receipt as proof that your client received my letter on xx/xx/xx. Your client did not provide the requested information. Instead, your client supplied copies of credit card statements which do not constitute Validation of Debt. Consequently, the time within which to respond to my request for validation has expired pursuant to the

above named Title and Section. The following court case which speaks of "…evidence sufficient to sustain its (creditor/plaintiff's) burden of proof", is for your reference:
In LVNV Funding, L.L.C. v. Colvell, 421 N.J.Super. 1 (App. Div. 2011), the Appellate Division reversed the trial court's grant of summary judgment for the plaintiff because plaintiff failed to submit evidence sufficient to sustain its burden of proof. Colvell involved the claim of Plaintiff on an allegedly defaulted credit card account. The opinion of the Court read in part: "In particular, when suing to collect the balance allegedly owed on an unpaid revolving credit card account, the creditor must prove more than merely the total amount remaining unpaid...the creditor must set forth the previous balance, and identify all transactions and credits, as well as the periodic rates, the balance on which the finance charge is computed, other charges, if any, the closing date of the billing cycle, and the new balance."

    At this time, I request that you stop all communications. I will log each call from you and document every collection letter from you and will consider each incident as a separate violation under FDCPA USC 1692g, SEC 813 (2-a) which carries a penalty of a maximum of $1000 for each violation. At this time I also inform you that if your offices have reported invalidated information to any of the 3 major Credit Bureau's (Equifax, Experian or TransUnion) this action might constitute fraud under both Federal and State Laws. Due to this fact, if any negative mark is found on any of my credit reports by your company or the company that you represent, I will not hesitate to seek legal counsel to bring legal action against you and demand penalties and punitive damages for your actions in violation of the aforementioned Title and Section.

Sincerely,

Card Holder's Signature
CARDHOLDER'S NAME
ADDRESS
CITY, STATE, ZIP
EMAILADDRESS: xxxxxx

****

Junk Debt Collectors Try to Collect on Old Judgments

If judgments have been entered against you in Court, it is not unusual for certain junk debt collectors to contact you and offer some type of settlement even if the judgments are very old. Remember, these collectors are bottom feeders and are hoping that your situation changed and you are in a better financial position today than when you defaulted on your alleged debts. They are hoping they can trick you into thinking that there is a benefit in satisfying the judgment at this particular juncture. There is really nothing to gain by indulging these bottom feeders. The judgments have been reported to credit reporting agencies and your FICO scores have already suffered. Even if your credit report shows "judgment satisfied", your FICO scores will only improve by a few points due to the fact that a creditor won a judgment against you. Moreover, how do you know the creditor will file a proper stipulation of settlement with the Court after you make the settlement payment you've agreed upon? The worst part is that the jurisdiction wherein the judgment was recorded may have a time limitation as to how long the judgment may appear in the public records. Some states delete judgments after only 7 years. If you make a payment to satisfy the judgment, the Court may republish the judgment due to the new transaction of satisfaction of the judgment, so it may reappear in public records again which is the last thing you want. My advice is to ignore these bottom feeding collectors if they are calling about an existing judgment recorded against you. But if you have some time and are really bored, you can have a little fun while learning something about the collection process. Write them this letter:

****

Date: xxxxxxxx
Certified Mail – Return Receipt Requested

Dear Collector:

I received your collection letter and telephone messages regarding the above-mentioned account. I would very much like to cooperate and possibly offer you a settlement but I need additional information. Please supply the following:

- Please name the Court and address of the Court where the judgment was recorded.
- Please state the name of the original creditor, the total amount of the judgment, the principal amount, interest and other charges such as legal fees and court costs that were added to the principal amount.
- Please provide a copy of your contract with the original creditor authorizing you to represent them in this matter. Provide proof that they contracted you to collect the outstanding judgment.
- If you bought the alleged debt from the original creditor, please provide a copy of the bill of sale.
- Supply proof that you are authorized to do business in my state. Provide a verifiable state license number, state tax registration and tax clearance showing that you are not in arrears in payment of any business taxes.

Your prompt response to the above request would be much appreciated.

Sincerely,

Card Holder's Signature
CARDHOLDER'S NAME
ADDRESS
CITY, STATE, ZIP
EMAILADDRESS: *xxxxxx*

****

After sending this letter, wait for a reply. But don't hold you breathe. The likelihood is you will never hear from this slimy bottom feeding collector again.

Why Creditors Prefer to Sue

To make it simple, for the sake of these discussions, we will refer to the credit card company and its collectors as "creditor" and/or "plaintiff" whether or not they sold your debt to a collection agency, junk debt buyer or collection attorney in your area. The methods and strategies will work the same way whomever you are dealing with. Let us review where we are. If you followed the instructions in Volume 1, a) you received satisfactory debt settlement offers from your creditors, b) unsatisfactory settlement offers or, c) you never heard back from some or any of your creditors. Congratulations if you received acceptable offers. Otherwise, the reason your negotiation-resistant creditors are resisting is that they may perceive they can collect more from you by holding out a little longer, by threatening to sue or by actually filing a lawsuit or an arbitration petition against you. This perception will diminish as soon as you convince them that your final offer of a settlement is the most they can recover from you. They will negotiate with you as soon as they come to the realization that you have the skill to squash every collection trick they try on you including their legal actions. That is why in any communications with them, which should always be in writing, you should sound like you know what you are talking about. If you sent your creditors 3 reminders urging them to answer your request for forgiveness but they have not replied, you must take action now before they file the lawsuit. You should first understand why they are resisting your request of forgiveness. They must think that they can easily win a judgment against you, i.e. you will not answer their Complaint when they file the suit in court and collect on the judgment due to information they have that leads them to believe that you have wages they can garnish and assets they can seize. They may also think that you are not insolvent and cannot file for bankruptcy protection, that your assets far exceed your liabilities. Most of the information comes from credit reporting agencies. These agencies collect not only credit information but personal information such as your employment history, public records, real estate owned, bank accounts and personal information about your spouse, ex-spouses and other close relatives. For this negotiation-resistance creditor you must keep reinforcing the idea that if they file suit against you, you will fight them. In the unlikely event they win (from the 1998 movie, "A CIVIL ACTION", Jan Schlichtmann played by John Travolta said: *"The odds of a plaintiff's lawyer winning in civil court are two to one against".*) they will not collect anything from you. You may be able to accomplish this by adding this paragraph at the end of every letter you send:

"If you choose to settle this matter in Court or through Arbitration, I caution you that you will spend a lot of money in legal fees. I will answer your Complaint with Motions and Demands for Production of Documents, Admissions, and Interrogatories. In the unlikely event that you succeed in obtaining a judgment against me, the judgment will be uncollectible. Because of my dire financial situation, I intend to file for bankruptcy protection upon notice that judgment against me is granted. This communication is provided solely for the purpose of notifying you to communicate in writing only and does not constitute an acknowledgement of the alleged debt shown above."

In my case, nothing serious happened until I had been delinquent for 120 days. I only received the usual reminders, collection letters and daily phone calls. The creditors became more aggressive after that, I believe due to my large balances and my algorithm that probably shows the creditors that I had the capability of making the minimum monthly payments. If I owed $5000 or less, I believe my creditors would not have been as aggressive. If it happens to you, you must take immediate action if the creditors' collection efforts intensify. If you start receiving many more collection calls at your residence or at your place of employment, final notices from collection agencies, threats of lawsuits from lawyers or letters by certified or registered mail, these are all signs that the creditor is getting serious in filing legal action against you. The Validation of Debt letter which also includes a cease and desist clause should give you a temporary relief from the creditor's collection activities. This is an important letter. It would be too late to send a Validation of Debt letter after your creditor files a lawsuit against you. You must send the Validation of Debt letter before a suit is filed. In any case, if a suit is filed, you must answer it or face a default judgment. A lawsuit filed against you will give the creditor the upper hand. You will have to either hire an attorney to help you answer the Complaint or spend a lot of time researching how to properly file an answer on your own as a pro-se (representing yourself) defendant. How will you answer the Complaint? What is your defense (or excuse) for not paying the bills? Therefore, you must send the Validation of Debt Letter the moment it becomes clear that the creditor will not accept your proposal for debt settlement. They may not tell you outright but the proof that they have rejected your proposal of settlement is that you never received a reply from them even after sending them 3 follow up letters, but they continue to send you dunning letters and threats of legal action.

There are many free examples of the Validation of Debt Letter in the internet but many of them are inadequate and many creditors found a way to respond to the request by providing insufficient information that they can argue constitutes validation of debt. For the debt validation request to be an effective tool for the debtor in order to force the creditor to reconsider debt settlement, it must contain a request for documents that most likely the creditor will not be able to provide. If the creditor responds to your request for validation of debt by enclosing copies of your 6 months' credit card statements, which is what they usually do as a reply to a validation of debt request, you must immediately send your response stating, *"....Thank you for your reply to my request for Validation of Debt. However, the enclosed copies of my statements do not fulfill your obligation to validate my alleged debt pursuant to the Fair Debt Collection Practices Act, 15 USC 1692g Sec. 809 (b). Please provide all the items requested on my letter within 10 days of receipt of this letter or indicate the reason for your failure to provide the requested information".* If they ignore your reply and file a lawsuit instead, you must answer their Complaint within the time required by the Court or face a default judgment. At this juncture, an opportunity opened up for you. After filing your answer to the Complaint (see sample Answer in this volume), you may file your own Motion for Summary Judgment against the creditor for its failure to validate your alleged debt, i.e. as a matter of law, the Plaintiff has no legal right to sue you in as much as they violated The Fair Debt Collection Practices Act, 15 USC 1692g Sec. 809 (b). Check with your Court how long you have to wait after filing your Answers to a Complaint before you can file a Motion for Summary Judgment against the Plaintiff. In some jurisdictions, you may file a Motion for Summary Judgment with your Answer to the Plaintiff's Complaint. A sample pleading for filing a Motion for Summary Judgment against the Plaintiff is shown towards the end of this book. It is a good idea to make 2 originals of the validation of debt letter and send one by regular first class mail and another one by certified mail. I have experienced in the past that some creditors and in particular many collection agencies either deliberately or unintentionally delay acceptance of certified mail. I have a sneaky suspicion that they know no certified mail is good news for them so they are not in a rush to retrieve it from the post office or accept it from the mailman. The debt validation letter shown below is very thorough and should create a problem for the creditor.

Please note that the second paragraph of the Validation of Debt letter relates specifically to my own personal case at the time it was written. You may delete it completely from the letter or you may add any grievance you may have concerning any unfair or questionable collection practices such as, "Your collector, Mr. Jones has been calling and leaving messages before 8am and after 9pm. Your collector has also been using abusive language and insults, impersonating an attorney, and informing third parties (such as neighbors, relatives, etc.) of my alleged debt. Each violation carries a penalty of $1000 pursuant to FDCPA, 15 USC 1692".

****

Validation of Debt, Cease and Desist Letter - Sample

By FIRST CLASS AND CERTIFIED MAIL RETURN RECEIPT REQUESTED
Date: xx/xx/xx
Name of Creditor, Collection Company or Law Firm
Address

RE: Account No.   xxxx xxxx xxxx $20,000

Dear Mr. or Ms. Xxxxxxxx (It is important to address your letter to the responsible person who sent you the collection letter)
This is a REQUEST for validation of debts.

This letter is being sent in reply to your enclosed collection letter dated xx/xx/xx a copy of which is attached.

This letter is also being sent to inform you that Tiffany from your office asked me for my checking account number to enable your offices to access my account and automatically take out payments for my alleged debt. She stated that my refusal to provide my checking account number will lead to payment of attorney's fees which could double the amount that I allegedly owe. Tiffany's notification violated 3 provisions of the FDCPA, 15 USC 1692. Each violation carries a penalty of $1000.

Be advised that this is not a refusal to pay, but a notice sent pursuant to the Fair Debt Collection Practices Act, 15 USC 1692g Sec. 809 (b) that your claim is disputed and validation is requested. This is NOT a request for "verification" or proof of my mailing address, but a request for VALIDATION made pursuant to the above named Title and Section. I respectfully request that your offices provide me with competent evidence that I have any legal obligation to pay you.

Please provide me with the following:

-What the money you say I owe is for;

-Explain and show me how you calculated what you say I owe;
-Provide me with receipts of the charges that equal the amount you say I owe;
-Provide me with copies of any papers that show I agreed to pay what you say I owe;
-Certified copy of my original credit application when I applied for your credit card;
-Provide a verification or copy of any judgment if applicable;
-Identify the original creditor;
-Prove the Statute of Limitations has not expired on this account;
-Show me that you are licensed to do business in my state. Provide your state license registration number and a copy of your certificate of good standing;
-Provide me with your Registered Agent's name and address.

At this time I will also inform you that if your offices have reported invalidated information to any of the 3 major Credit Bureau's (Equifax, Experian or TransUnion) this action might constitute fraud under both Federal and State Laws. Due to this fact, if any negative mark is found on any of my credit reports by your company or the company that you represent I will not hesitate in bringing legal action against you for the following:

Violation of the Fair Credit Reporting Act
Violation of the Fair Debt Collection Practices Act
Defamation of Character

If your offices are able to provide the proper documentation as requested in the aforementioned Declaration, I will require at least 30 days to investigate this information and during such time all collection activity must cease and desist. Also during this validation period, if any action is taken which could be considered detrimental to any of my credit reports, I will consult with my legal counsel for suit. This includes listing of any information to a credit reporting repository that could be inaccurate or invalidated or verifying an account as accurate when in fact there is no provided proof that it is.

If your offices fail to respond to this validation request within 30 days from the date of your receipt, all references to this account must be deleted and completely removed from my credit file and a copy of such deletion request shall be sent to me immediately.

This letter will also serve as my written request that no telephone contact be made by your offices to my home or to my place of employment. Please be informed that my employer does not allow calls from collection agencies or creditors. If your offices attempt telephone communication with me, including but not limited to computer generated calls and calls or correspondence sent to or with any third parties, it will be considered harassment and I will have no choice but to file suit. All future communications with me MUST be done in writing and sent to the address noted in this letter by USPS certified mail return receipt requested. Also, please be reminded that each violation to my request to cease and desist carries a civil liability of $1000 for each occurrence in accordance with FDCPA, 15 USC 1692k Sec. 813. Be informed that I will document every violation by logging each call received from your offices.

It would be advisable that you assure that your records are in order before I am forced to take legal action. This is an attempt to correct your records, any information obtained shall be used for that purpose.

Sincerely,

Card Holder's Signature
CARDHOLDER'S NAME
ADDRESS
CITY, STATE, ZIP
EMAILADDRESS: xxxxxx

****

When Creditor Ignores Validation of Debt Letter

If you do not receive a reply for validation of debt within 30 days, but continue to receive calls and collection letters, you should write the follow up letter below:
****

By FIRST CLASS AND CERTIFIED MAIL RETURN RECEIPT REQUESTED
Date: xx/xx/xx
Name of Creditor, Collection Company or Law Firm
Address

RE: Account No. xxxx xxxx xxxx $20,000

Dear Mr. or Ms. or Attorney Xxxxxxxxx: (It is important to address the letter to the responsible person, the one who sent you the most recent collection letter or final notice)

A validation of debt was requested on xx/xx/xx. The request was received by a certain Mr. or Ms. (Name of receiver) of (Creditor, Collection Agency, Law Office) on xx/xx/xxxx (date), as per the enclosed postal receipt. Validation was never provided and the time within which to provide such validation in accordance with FDCPA USC 1692g, SEC 809 (b) has expired. You have waived your right to collect this debt. Therefore you must cease collection of this alleged debt in accordance with the Fair Debt Collection Practices Act. Please advise all the reporting agencies to delete any references to this alleged debt. Your failure to do so will subject your company to severe penalties under the FDCPA rules. Furthermore, should you decide to file a Complaint against me, I will cite your failure to provide timely validation of debt as one of my affirmative defenses.

Additionally, please do not refer this matter to a different collection agency. You and your assigns could be subjected to penalties of $1000 for each violation in accordance with FDCPA USC 1692g, SEC 813 (2-a).

Sincerely,

Card Holder's Signature
CARDHOLDER'S NAME
ADDRESS
CITY, STATE, ZIP
EMAILADDRESS: xxxxxx

****

The above letter will drive the point to your creditor that winning a lawsuit against you will not be a cakewalk. This is where they have to make a business decision of whether or not they can justify the amount of work they have to put into your case for the amount of money they think they can eventually collect from you.

In my case, a smart aleck lawyer replied to my request for Validation of Debt by simply attaching the credit card company's statement to my letter. It prompted me to write the following letter:
****

By FIRST CLASS AND CERTIFIED MAIL RETURN RECEIPT REQUESTED
Date: xx/xx/xx
Name of Creditor, Collection Company or Law Firm
Address
Dear Attorney Xxxxxxxxxx:
RE: Account No. xxxx xxxx xxxx $20,000
I received your response to my request for Validation of Debt and thank you for a copy of my statement. Please be informed that the statement of account does not satisfy my request for Validation of Debt. A copy of my debt validation

request is attached. A case reference is shown below for your review:

In LVNV Funding, L.L.C. v. Colvell, 421 N.J.Super. 1 (App. Div. 2011), the Appellate Division reversed the trial court's grant of summary judgment for the plaintiff because plaintiff failed to submit evidence sufficient to sustain its burden of proof. Colvell involved the claim of Plaintiff on an allegedly defaulted credit card account. The opinion of the Court read in part: "In particular, when suing to collect the balance allegedly owed on an unpaid revolving credit card account, the creditor must prove more than merely the total amount remaining unpaid. ...the creditor must set forth the previous balance, and identify all transactions and credits, as well as the periodic rates, the balance on which the finance charge is computed, other charges, if any, the closing date of the billing cycle, and the new balance."

Once again, please supply copies of all the requested documents within 30 days. If I do not receive the documents within 30 days, I will assume that you have waived your right to collect this alleged debt. Therefore, you must cease collection of this alleged debt in accordance with the Fair Debt Collection Practices Act. Please advise all the reporting agencies to delete any references to this alleged debt.

If you decide to bring an action against me in court, this letter will be used in support of my Answer to your Complaint. Furthermore, my Answer will include a counter-suit for violations of FDCPA provisions, USC 1692g, SEC 805 to 808.

Please be guided accordingly.
Sincerely,

Card Holder's Signature
CARDHOLDER'S NAME
ADDRESS
CITY, STATE, ZIP

Creditors May Sue in Court or File for an Arbitration Hearing

Instead of negotiating settlement of my debt or filing a lawsuit in a competent court, one of my creditors filed for arbitration proceedings against me. Arbitration is an alternative dispute resolution which is more informal and supposedly faster and cheaper (for the petitioner) than filing a suit in Court. However, I have some familiarity with the rules of the Court due to my experience in the corporate environment but I knew next to nothing about Arbitration proceedings so I did a little research while contemplating the next move. What I discovered is that many corporations prefer arbitration to litigation in a civil court. They have a definite advantage over the consumer and the case falls into the hands of only one arbitrator who might as well be called the judge, the jury…and executioner. Is that fair for you, the consumer/debtor? I don't think so. Many arbitrators are lawyers who represent businesses like the credit card companies, banks and other consumer loan providers. I was surprised to learn that arbitrators do not have to follow the law but instead can make decisions based on what they perceive to be fair rather than what the law directs. If I went along with it, the arbitrator gets to decide my fate instead of a panel of jurors whom I think are likely to be more biased towards one of their peers. Finally, arbitration awards are almost never reversed and are enforceable just like judgments. I called my creditor's attorney and asked him why he filed a Petition for Arbitration instead of a Complaint in Court and he told me that I agreed to settle any disputes through mandatory arbitration. He informs me further that the credit card company inserted a notice for mandatory arbitration agreement in one of their monthly statements that states: "…any disputes shall be resolved through binding arbitration…" The fact that the credit card company never received any objection from me meant I agreed. If this happens to you, write the following letter:

****

Refusal of Arbitration

By FIRST CLASS AND CERTIFIED MAIL RETURN RECEIPT REQUESTED

Date: xx/xx/xx

Name of Law Firm
Address

RE: Account No. xxxx xxxx xxxx $20,000, File#
Arbitration Case No. - xxxxxxxxxxx

Dear Attorney Xxxxxxxx: (It is important to address this letter to the attorney in charge of this case)

    I am in receipt of your Arbitration Petition and this is to inform you that I hereby refuse and object to participation in any arbitration proceeding for the following reasons:
(1) There were no existing or legitimate disputes between the parties at the time the claimant made the attempt to include any arbitration provision in any purported agreements.
    (A) Additionally, if this clause was part of any original written agreements between the parties, it violates House Resolution 5162 which amends Title 15 USC 1601 of the Consumer Credit Protection Act.
    (B) It also violates amendments to the Federal Arbitration Act (S. 192) which make pre-dispute mandatory arbitration agreements in consumer credit contracts invalid and unenforceable.
    (C) Additionally, H.R. 1054 and 3607 that amend the Truth in Lending Act make pre-dispute mandatory arbitration agreements between a lender and consumer void and unenforceable.

(2) In addition, any arbitration forums chosen by the claimant are unfair and, unconstitutionally violate respondent's rights to due process and they constitute an unfair trade practice.
(A) "The arbitration agreement in a credit cardholder agreement is unconscionable and unenforceable, to the extent it prohibits class treatment of small individual claims, where presented as a 'take it or leave it' clause with no opportunity for negotiation" Szetela v. Discover Bank, No. G029323 (Cal. 4th App. Dist. April 22, 2002)

(B)The purported arbitration clause is not enforceable because it unconscionably requires the respondent to arbitrate in a distant state under an organization and rules designed to favor the purported lender.
(a)Patterson v ITT Consumer Financial Corp., 14 Cal. App. 4th 1659, 18 Cal Rptr 2d 563 (Cal App. 1993) "The claimant has no authority to unilaterally change any terms of any agreements that may or may not exist between the claimant and respondent. The post-agreement, unilateral arbitration clause is unenforceable because it exceeds the unilateral right of one party to make subsequent, substantive, changes to the agreement, violates the implied covenant of good faith and fair dealing and because the resulting jury waiver was not unambiguous and unequivocal, as required to waive a constitutional right."
(3) Furthermore, mandatory arbitration may not be imposed without the MEANINGFUL consent of BOTH parties.

(A)The United States Supreme Court has repeatedly stressed that arbitration under the [Federal Arbitration Act (F.A.A.)] is a matter of consent, not coercion.
(a)Allied-Bruce Terminex Co. v. Dobson (1995) 513 U.S. 265, 270;
(b)First Options of Chicago, Inc. v. Kaplan (1995) 514 U.S. 938, 944;
(c)Mastrobuono v. Shearson Lehman Hutton, Inc. (1995) 514 U.S. 52, 55-56;

(d) Volt Info. Sciences, Inc. v. Board of Trustees (1989) 489 U.S. 468, 478.

(e) AT&T Tech., Inc. v. Communications Workers (1986) 475 U.S. 643, 648:

(4) A party cannot be required to submit to arbitration to any dispute which he has not agreed so to submit. Therefore, I refuse to accept arbitration and dispute your claim in its entirety.

Sincerely,

Card Holder's Signature
CARDHOLDER'S NAME
ADDRESS
CITY, STATE, ZIP
EMAILADDRESS: *xxxxxx*
Cc: Arbitration Clerk
****

Make sure to mail the letter to the attorney and send a copy to the Arbitration clerk by certified mail return receipt requested. The likelihood is that you will receive a notice of dismissal of Claimant's petition. In the unlikely event that the creditor/petitioner receives an award without your participation and files a Confirmation of Award in a competent court, you may file a motion to dismiss and vacate the Arbitration Award. This will be further discussed in Volume 3 of this series.

The attorney's next move would either be an attempt to go back to negotiating a settlement of your debt or file a lawsuit. If they want to negotiate settlement, start with offering them 5% of the original amount on your statement when you first wrote the letter and go as high as 15% if you can afford it.

If they decide to sue, you will receive a standard Summons and Complaint similar to the one below:
****

Creditor/Plaintiff's Complaint

LAW OFFICE
ADDRESS
CREDITOR'S NAME, Plaintiff

NAME OF COURT
Docket NO.
COMPLAINT

Vs.
YOUR NAME, Defendant

Plaintiff, xxxxxxxxxxxx (Creditor) by way of Complaint against the Defendant says:

First Count: There is due from the Defendant to the Plaintiff the sum of $20,000, on a certain book account, a true copy of which is annexed hereto as Schedule "A" (they probably attached a copy of your last statement of account or an affidavit of debt from an employee of the creditor/plaintiff). Payment has been demanded and has not been made.

Second Count: Defendant obtained a credit card from Plaintiff.

Third Count: Defendant used the credit card to obtain goods and services.

Fourth Count: The Defendant, being indebted to the Plaintiff in the sum of $20,000 upon an account stated between them, did promise to pay to the Plaintiff said sum upon demand. Payment has been demanded and has not been made.

It is important to answer the Complaint within the time required in the Summons, usually 20 to 30 days from the date of receipt of the Summons and Complaint, depending on the jurisdiction. If you ignore the Complaint, the creditor/plaintiff may apply for a default judgment against you. Most Courts have a standard pre-printed form or template for answering a Plaintiff's Complaint and you should transcribe your Answer onto that template. Definitions of affirmative defenses came from a legal dictionary and are followed by brief explanations.

Below is a sample Defendant's Answer to Plaintiff's Complaint. Make sure to use the acceptable "Answer to Complaint" form that should be available through your County Court Clerk:

****

Sample Answer to Complaint

YOUR NAME – *Pro Se* (This is a term to signify you are representing yourself in this case)
YOUR ADDRESS
PHONE NUMBER

CREDITOR'S NAME, Plaintiff

                              NAME OF COURT
                              Division of Court
                              Docket NO.
                              DEFENDANT'S
Vs.   ANSWER AND
                              AFFIRMATIVE
                              DEFENSES

YOUR NAME, Defendant

    Defendant, as and for his/her Answer and Affirmative Defenses to the Complaint in this matter, respectfully represents and alleges as follows:

    First Count: The allegations represent a statement of claims of the pleader, and as such, do not require a response. However, to the extent a response is required, the allegations in this paragraph are denied.

    Second Count: The allegations represent a statement of claims of the pleader, and as such, do not require a response. However, to the extent a response is required, the allegations in this paragraph are denied. No agreement has been submitted into the record to evidence the allegation and leaves Plaintiff to provide proof.

    Third Count: The allegations represent a statement of claims of the pleader, and as such, do not require a response. However, to the extent a response is required, the allegations in this paragraph are denied. No evidence has been submitted into the record to support allegation.

      Fourth Count: The allegations represent a statement of claims of the pleader, and as such, do not require a response. However, to the extent a response is required, the allegations in this paragraph are denied. The Plaintiff is making an unsupported statement that a contract or agreement exists. No agreement has been submitted into the record to evidence the allegation. The Plaintiff's statement is based on hearsay.

AFFIRMATIVE DEFENSES
First Affirmative Defense: The Complaint fails to state a claim upon which relief may be granted.

Second Affirmative Defense: Plaintiff's claim is barred due to violation of the Fair Debt Collection Practices Act, 15 USC 1692e Sec.809 (b). Plaintiff refused Defendant's request for validation of debt (attach copies of debt validation request and follow up letters-Exhibits, 1 to 5) or otherwise failed to validate debt within the time prescribed by law.

Third Affirmative Defense: Plaintiff's claims are barred by the doctrine of laches.

Fourth Affirmative Defense: Plaintiff's claims are barred by the doctrine of waiver.

Fifth Affirmative Defense: Plaintiff's claims are barred by the doctrine of unclean hands.

      Wherefore, Defendant demands judgment dismissing Plaintiff's Complaint with prejudice; and for such other relief as this Court deems just and proper.

Dated: _____   by: Your Name, Defendant

****

DEFINITIONS AND EXPLANATIONS:

Affirmative defense 1 simply means that the Plaintiff did not state a particular state law that was violated.

Affirmative defense 2 means that Plaintiff has been unable to validate the alleged debt.

Affirmative defenses 3 to 5 are common defenses that can easily be alleged and often proven against the creditor, collector or junk debt holder. I include them in answers to Complaints. Citing the defenses may prompt the Plaintiff to search for deficiencies in their Complaint and review their actions prior to filing the Complaint. In my experience, I did not supplement the affirmative defenses with proper case law citations and statutory references to applicable laws and court rulings but the lack of references and citations to these defenses did not do any harm.

The brief definitions of these doctrines shown below came from a legal dictionary, and examples based on my experience follow the definitions:

Doctrine of Laches

Based on the maxim that equity aids the vigilant and not those who procrastinate regarding their rights; Neglect to assert a right or claim that, together with lapse of time and other circumstances, prejudices an adverse party. Neglecting to do what should or could, have been done to assert a claim or right for an unreasonable and unjustified time causing disadvantage to another. Laches is similar to 'statute of limitations' except is equitable rather than statutory and is a common affirmative defense raised in civil actions. In general, when a party has been guilty of laches in enforcing his right by great delay and lapse of time, this circumstance will at common law prejudice and sometimes operate in bar of a remedy which is discretionary for the court to afford. In courts of equity delay will also generally be prejudicial.

Doctrine of Waiver
The relinquishment or refusal to accept of a right. In practice it is required of every one to take advantage of his rights at a proper time and, neglecting to do so, will be considered as a waiver. If, for example, a defendant who has been misnamed in the writ and declaration, pleads over, he cannot afterwards take advantage of the error by pleading in abatement, for his plea amounts to a waiver. In contracts, if, after knowledge of a supposed fraud, surprise or mistake, a party performs the agreement in part, he will be considered as having waived the objection. It is a rule of the civil law, consonant with reason that any one may renounce or waive that which has been established in his favor.

Doctrine of Unclean Hands
A legal doctrine which is a defense to a Complaint, which states that a party who is asking for a judgment cannot have the help of the court if he/she has done anything unethical in relation to the subject of the lawsuit. Thus, if a defendant can show the plaintiff had "unclean hands," the plaintiff's Complaint will be dismissed or the plaintiff will be denied judgment. Unclean hands is a common "affirmative defense" pleaded by defendants, which must be proved by the defendant.

This is the way I used **Doctrine of Laches** in my particular case: Delays in bringing suit and in refusing to negotiate alleged debt of defendant intentionally preventing defendant from responding to an offer or acceptance resulting in prejudice to defendant. If after all, you have to appear before a judge in a hearing and are asked to explain your reason for citing this doctrine as a defense, you may simply say "Judge, I sent the plaintiff a letter that I am willing to negotiate even though they have not validated my alleged debt, but they chose not to respond and it took them a year to file a lawsuit to my detriment. I have been prejudiced because of the long time it has taken."

When asked about **Doctrine of Waiver**, I replied this way: "Your Honor, I sent a request for validation of debt and never heard back from plaintiff. It seems to me that they have waived their right to validate debt. Plaintiff's collector informed me that they cannot validate my alleged debt. That is why I included this doctrine as an affirmative defense."

With regard to **Doctrine of Unclean Hands Defense**, this can be a recitation of any unethical collection methods the creditor/plaintiff used. In my case I replied this way, "Judge, plaintiff's collector falsely represented himself to be an attorney in our conversation of xx/xx/xx. Plaintiff's employee continued to communicate with me even after being notified to cease communications in violation of FDCPA rules."

Check with the court clerk or open your state's website for the rules of civil procedure to find out what the filing fee is and what other necessary legal documents must be included with your Answer to Plaintiff's Complaint. In my state the following documents must be included for first pleaders:

-CIVIL CASE INFORMATION STATEMENT (Court Clerk can provide a pre-printed form)

-CERTIFICATION OF COMPLIANCE WITH RULE REGARDING REDACTION OF PERSONAL INFORMATION. In my state, this statement must be included in the pleading, at the bottom of the Answer to Complaint, "I certify that confidential personal identifiers have been redacted from documents now submitted to the Court and will be redacted from all documents submitted in the future in accordance with the rules of the Court."

-CERTIFICATION THAT THE MATTER IN CONTROVERSY IS NOT SUBJECT TO ANY OTHER ACTION. Sample below:

CERTIFICATION

Pursuant to the provisions of this court, the undersigned certifies that this matter is not the subject of any other action pending in any court or arbitration proceeding, nor is any other action or arbitration proceeding contemplated, and all known necessary parties have been joined in this action.

Dated: by: Your Name,
                                            Defendant

****

CERTIFICATION OF MAILING. Sample below:
<u>CERTIFICATION of MAILING</u>

I hereby certify that on _____, I served the Plaintiff true copies of the following by certified mail:

-Civil Case Information Statement
-Answer and Affirmative Defenses
-Filing Fee, Check No. Xxxxxxxx
-First Request for Production of Documents (Sample after this section)

The copies were addressed to the Plaintiff at the following mailing address:

1. LAW OFFICES OF Xxxxxxxx
ADDRESS
2. ORIGINAL CREDITOR'S NAME
ADDRESS

Date: _____   by: Your Name,
                                             Defendant

****

States have different requirements for service of "Answer to Complaint". Some states require a third party to issue the Certification of Mailing or Affidavit of Service. Some states require the Affidavit or Certification to be notarized. Check with the county court clerk for the procedures for filing your "Answer to Complaint". Serve a copy of the package to the plaintiff by certified mail then wait until you receive the green postal receipt from the addressees signifying that they have been served with your Answer to the Complaint. Then mail the original package and two sets of copies to the court by certified mail. Make sure to include the check for the filing fee. The court clerk may send you a notification that your Answer has been filed or may return the entire package indicating that there is a mistake or deficiency in your documents. In most cases, you can call the court clerk for further clarification if there is a deficiency. In a state such as Minnesota, a civil lawsuit can be maintained outside the court system for a year. The plaintiff may send you "an unfiled Complaint" and compel you to go through the process of discovery, e.g. Interrogatories, Request for Admissions and Production of Documents, etc. etc., without actually filing the lawsuit in court. If they do not file the suit in court within a year, the case is automatically dismissed with prejudice.

More Sample Complaints and Answers

The following are variations of Plaintiff/Creditor's Complaint followed by my answers:

1. Defendant owes Plaintiff $20,000 for goods and services sold and delivered to Defendant and/or by receiving a cash advance or balance transfer. Said purchases were made on Defendant's charge account bearing account number xxxxxxxxxxxx which was issued to Defendant by Capital One Bank.

Answer: Denied. No evidence has been submitted into the record to support the allegation. The Plaintiff's statement is based on hearsay.

2. Defendant is in default for failing to make the required payments on the charge account under the agreement and now owes the plaintiff the sum of $20,000.

Answer: Denied. No agreement has been submitted into the record to evidence the allegation and leaves Plaintiff to provide proof. The plaintiff's complaint indicates the existence of a Consumer Credit Contract that was not attached to the Complaint and defendant requests copies of all contracts, assignments and sale agreements pertaining to the alleged account. The Plaintiff is making an unsupported statement that a contract or agreement exists without providing an account agreement or details regarding the alleged account. Defendant demands strict proof thereof. The plaintiff has failed to establish proof of ownership of the alleged account and has not proven a standing to sue.

Then there are many other declarations that lawyers include in their pleadings that can confuse the defendant. In most jurisdictions the defendant is required to provide an answer to all the allegations or the defendant's answer to the plaintiff's complaint may be deemed by the judge as incomplete and plaintiff may file a "Motion to Quash Defendant's Answers" which can put the defendant in default of answering the Plaintiff's Complaint. One example of such declaration/allegation is shown below:

1. Bank of America, N.A. ("BANA") is a wholly-owned subsidiary of Bank of America Corporation and the successor-in-interest to FIA Card Services, formerly known as MBNA American Bank (FIA). FIA was merged into and under the charter and title of BANA effective October 1, 2014.

If you are a Pro-se defendant (you have no attorney) as I was, the above declaration/allegation will confuse the heck out of you. First thing that came to mind is that, it must be a legal trick. After doing research, I came up with the answer below:

Answer: Defendant has insufficient information to admit or deny plaintiff's statement and leaves Plaintiff to provide proof.

The following are other variations of wordings of allegations you may see in a Complaint and various answers you should provide:

- This is an action for damages for $xxxxxxx

ANSWER: The allegation represents a statement of the pleader, and as such does not require a response. However, to the extent a response is required, Defendant lacks sufficient information to either admit or deny Plaintiff's allegation. Plaintiff is requested to provide, statute, case law, or custom to support its allegation.

- Plaintiff and Defendant had business transactions between them and they agreed to the resulting balance.

ANSWER: Denied. No proof has been submitted into the record to evidence the allegation and leaves Plaintiff to provide proof.

- The Defendant made purchases of various and diverse consumer goods and/or effected cash advances through the use of a credit account obtained from the Plaintiff on account number xxxxxxxx.

ANSWER: Denied. No original card agreement has been submitted into the record to evidence the allegation and leaves Plaintiff to provide proof. The Complaint indicates the existence of a Consumer Credit Card Contract that was not attached to the Complaint and Defendant requests copies of all contracts, amendments, assignments and sale agreements pertaining to the alleged account; and that Defendant received, approved and signed the aforementioned documents from the Plaintiff.

- Plaintiff rendered a statement of account to Defendant and Defendant did not object to the statement.

ANSWER: Denied. Plaintiff alleges the doctrine, "Account Stated" as a cause of action in this Complaint and therefore must provide the following proof:

a) *That a statement of account was mailed to the Defendant and that Defendant held the statement for an unreasonable amount of time without objection;*
b) *That Defendant received the statement;*
c) *That Defendant did not object to the balance shown on the statement.*

Another confusing declaration in a Complaint followed by my answers:

- Venue for this action is proper in this Court because the Defendant is a resident of this county. Or, Defendant is an adult individual residing in this county.

ANSWER: These are questions which you can readily Admit or Deny. Do not plead, "lack of information" or the judge may see right through you and may decide you are playing games and may just throw out your Answer. If the statement is true, admit it.

Request for Production of Documents

To assert your right to seek information that you are entitled to in accordance with the law, it is a good idea to submit a Request for Production of Documents with your Answer to the Complaint. A sample is shown below:

YOUR NAME
ADDRESS
PHONE NO.
Pro Se

CREDITOR'S NAME, Plaintiff

                            NAME OF COURT
                            Division of Court
                            Docket NO.
Vs.   DEFENDANT'S
                            FIRST REQUEST
                            FOR PRODUCTION
                            OF DOCUMENTS

YOUR NAME, Defendant

TO: LAW OFFICE (Plaintiff or Plaintiff's Lawyer)
     ADDRESS

SIRS:

PLEASE TAKE NOTICE, that pursuant to the rules of the Court, demand is hereby made that the Plaintiff produce the following documents within the time prescribed by law:

1 Copies of any signed agreement(s) between Plaintiff and Defendant.

2 Copies of any and all correspondence received from me bearing my signature.

3 Proof of authority of plaintiff to conduct business in the state of xxxxxxxxxxxx, such as, copy of state license, certificate of good standing, name of registered agent and address of registered agent.

4 Certified true copy of Defendant's credit card application bearing defendant's signature.

5 Copies of contracts or agreements proving that collectors who have ever communicated with me to collect alleged debt are authorized agents of the original creditor.

6 Copies of signed credit card charges that equal the amount of my alleged debt.

Dated: _____   Your Name,
                                Defendant

****

Let us summarize where we are at this point. You received a Summons and Complaint from the creditor/plaintiff and you prepared the following documents and mailed them by certified mail within the time indicated on the summons:
-Answer and Affirmative Defenses to Complaint

-First Request for Production of Documents
-Filing Fee, Check No. _____, Amount $____
-Other certifications and forms required by the Court (Check with the Court Clerk or go to your state's website for Rules of Civil Procedure).

     In my experience, at this point of the litigation, it is better NOT to file a counter-claim, also known as counter-suit for any violations of the FDCPA. If the Court assigns a hearing (aka Pre-Trial Conference) date and the Plaintiff cannot produce evidence by that time, chances are plaintiff will abandon the case and will not appear for the hearing, thereby leaving you to move for dismissal with prejudice. However, if you file a counter-suit, plaintiff is more likely to make an appearance, find a way to request a trial and defend the counter-suit as his non-appearance could win you a default judgment against him for the amount shown on your counter-suit. You will be put at a great disadvantage if the creditor's attorney makes an appearance. He is more familiar with the rules of civil procedure than you are. This is what he does for a living and he will be mad as hell for being forced to appear to defend the counter-suit. He will not waste his time to appear if he thinks he cannot win his case, but will have to if he has to defend against a counter-claim.

     If your legal package has no mistakes, you will receive a "filed notice" from the court and the court may set the date of the hearing. There is a difference between a hearing and a trial. A hearing is a short procedure whereby the parties go before a judge and can present their side orally and offer evidence and get a chance to dispute the other party's argument and evidence. A judge can make a preliminary analysis of the case and can decide if there is even a case that should go to trial. If the judge decides there is a case, the case goes to trial where there is a formal proceeding either before a jury or before a bench judge who will hand down the verdict. If the creditor/plaintiff cannot produce the evidence requested in your Request for Production of Documents, the case may go to a hearing but will not likely go to a trial, unless the plaintiff's attorney finds a legal way of trying the case without valid proof or evidence. In most cases, if the case goes through a hearing, when your case is called and both parties are present, the judge will ask both parties to see a mediator in one of the small rooms or hallway of the court to see if the opposing parties can come to an agreement. The plaintiff's attorney and sometimes with the help of the mediator (in my experience with these types of cases) will try to convince you that you have no chance of winning and you should settle. Do not be intimidated. If you followed the steps correctly, the law is on your side. The law dictates that the plaintiff has no case if they failed to validate your alleged debts within 30 days. The burden of proof is on the plaintiff to produce the documents you have requested.

If you reject the mediator and the attorney's settlement offer, which in most cases is for you to pay the full amount, and opt to go in front of the judge instead, the following may occur:
- The plaintiff will present his case first. If plaintiff appears without the evidence requested in your Request for Production of Documents, when it is your turn to speak, request the judge to throw out the case by saying, "Your Honor, I move for dismissal of Plaintiff's case with prejudice for lack of evidence." If plaintiff produces a copy of your credit application and copies of signed credit card charges you can say, "Judge, although the signatures look like mine, how can anyone prove I really signed them? We need to see the original documents with my signature in ink on all the documents."
-If you appear in court and the plaintiff is a "no show", you can request the judge to throw out the case by saying, "Judge, I move for dismissal of this case with prejudice."
-The Plaintiff may request for an adjournment by telling the court that they need more time to produce requested documents. Unless you object, the court will grant the adjournment and may or may not set a new hearing date. If the court does not set a new date, plaintiff may just abandon the case or sell or resell your

debt to another collector or junk debt buyer. You may object by saying, "Judge, I object to giving the plaintiff more time to produce evidence. It has been over 100 days since my request for production. They have failed to validate my alleged debt and they have failed to produce the documents I've requested. I move for dismissal of the case with prejudice."

-If you have not received the requested documents from the plaintiff as the hearing date draws near, another option for you is to request for an adjournment of the hearing if you do not want to go to court. Make sure you do this 2 weeks before the hearing date not 1 or 2 days before the hearing. Call the plaintiff's attorney to see if he will agree to adjourn on the grounds that they have not provided the requested documents and you are willing to give them more time. Then you have to call the Court Clerk or write the Court the following letter:

****

RE: Docket No._____, Plaintiff's Name vs. Your Name
Dear Clerk of the Court:

I am the defendant in the above entitled case. I have the consent and agreement of the plaintiff to request adjournment of this case until such time that plaintiff is able to produce the documents requested in my Request for Production of Documents dated _____.
Respectfully,

Signature
NAME *xxxxxxx*, *Defendant*
ADDRESS
CITY, STATE, ZIP
EMAILADDRESS: *xxxxxxx*
Cc: Plaintiff

****

Collection attorneys know all the tricks in book so they may reject your request for adjournment in the hope that they can force you to settle right there and then. Your request for adjournment may give them the impression that you are afraid to appear in court so they may bluff their way into forcing you to settle and I can just imagine that they will take a tougher stance on the amount they will accept as final settlement at this point. If this happens to you, your only choice is to call their bluff and say you will go to the hearing but they better bring the documents listed on your Request for Production of Documents or you will move for a dismissal with prejudice. If you get their consent for an adjournment, it may give you a temporary relief but your problem may not go away. It may rear its ugly head again if they sell your alleged debt (again) to another (tougher) junk debt buyer. The miserable collection process can start anew until the debt becomes "time-barred" due to the statute of limitation.

There are other legal ways to get a dismissal with prejudice by filing motions for failure of Plaintiff to serve timely answers to Defendant's Interrogatories, Requests for Admissions and Production of Documents. These are discussed in Volume 3 of this series. I have not recommended propounding interrogatories and request for admissions because it opens up the likelihood that the plaintiff will propound its own interrogatories and request for admissions. Answering their interrogatories under oath can put you, the debtor in a vulnerable position. For example, they will definitely ask: "Did you apply for a credit card…; did you use your credit card to purchase or charge..." Lying under oath is perjury and can land you in jail. But there ways to answer these questions without lying. More of this and how to answer plaintiff's interrogatories and request for admissions in volume 3 of this series.

Creditor/Plaintiff's Motion for Summary Judgment

If the creditor/plaintiff's attorney is a seasoned veteran and skilled in collections as the lawyer was in my case, he can file a Motion for Summary Judgment. This is the debtor/defendant's worst nightmare. Ordinary citizens who are not familiar with civil court procedures would not know how to deal with it. In my case, the plaintiff's attorney filed the motion with a standard pre-printed form essentially saying: "Plaintiff moves for summary judgment on the grounds that there is no genuine issue as to any material fact and Plaintiff is entitled to judgment as a matter of law."

If you receive the notice of Motion for Summary Judgment, don't panic but make sure to file your opposition to the Motion before the deadline stated on the notice or Judgment against you may be granted. Upon receipt of the notice from my creditor's counsel, I did a quick research and constructed my opposition as follows:

****

YOUR NAME
YOUR ADDRESS
YOUR PHONE NO.
Pro Se

CREDITOR'S NAME, Plaintiff

Vs.

OPPOSING MOTION FOR SUMMARY JUDGMENT

YOUR NAME, Defendant

    NAME OF COURT
    Division of Court
    Docket NO.
    DEFENDANT'S CERTIFICATION

Defendant, "YOUR NAME" upon his/her certification, says:

1) I hereby make this certification opposing plaintiff's motion which I received on xx/xx/xxxx.

In Judson v. People's Bank and Trust Co. of Westfield, 17 N.J. 67, 74 (1954) Justice William Brennan described the test to be employed by the Trial Court in evaluating whether the Trial Court should grant or deny a Motion for Summary Judgment filed pursuant to R. 4:46-2. Justice Brennan observed that the Summary Judgment procedure,

"…is designed to provide a prompt, business like and inexpensive method of disposing of any cause which a discriminating search of the merits and pleadings, depositions and admissions on file, together with the affidavits submitted on the motion clearly shows not to present any genuine issue of material fact requiring disposition at trial...The Summary Judgment procedure aims at the swift uncovering of the merits and either their effective disposition or their advancement towards prompt resolution by trial...."

2) Plaintiff has not presented any material facts to support its claim. Plaintiff has failed to produce the documents in my Request for Production of Documents dated _____. The purpose of discovery is to seek the truth so that disputes may be decided by what the facts reveal, not by what the facts conceal.

3) Plaintiff's reply to my request for production of documents is a series of printed matter which does not explain the plaintiff's claim and which does not bear any defendant's signature.

4) In the matter of Brill v. Guardian Life Ins. Co. of America, 142 N.J. 520, 536 (1995) which says in part,

(Summary judgment may be appropriate when the evidence) "is so one-sided that one party must prevail as a matter of law."

In this case, the plaintiff has not provided any evidence, and in fact has violated Federal FDCPA Section 809, (15USC 1692g) which says in part "...if the consumer notifies the debt collector in writing within 30 days that the debt, or any portion thereof, is disputed, the debt collector will obtain verification of the debt.......and a copy of such verification will be mailed to the consumer by the debt collector...."

5) Respectfully, based on the foregoing, plaintiff's motion for summary judgment should be denied and discovery should proceed in accordance with rules of the Court.

6) I certify that the foregoing statements made by me are true. I am aware that if any of the foregoing statements made by me are willfully false, I am subject to punishment.

Dated: _____   *Signature*
NAME xxxxxxx, Defendant
ADDRESS
CITY, STATE, ZIP
EMAILADDRESS: xxxxxx

****

The preceding Opposition should be mailed with the following Certification of Mailing (Affidavit of Service) as required by civil court procedure in your state:

****

YOUR NAME
YOUR ADDRESS

YOUR PHONE NO.
Pro Se

CREDITOR'S NAME, Plaintiff

                      NAME OF COURT
                      Division of Court
                      Docket NO.

Vs.

                      CERTIFICATION
                      OF MAILING

YOUR NAME, Defendant

I hereby certify that on____day of _____, _____, I served true copies of the following by first class and certified mail:

    CERTIFICATION OPPOSING MOTION
    FOR SUMMARY JUDGMENT

The copies were addressed to the plaintiff at the following mailing address:

    CREDITOR/PLAINTIFF'S LAWYER
    ADDRESS

cc: ORIGINAL CREDITOR'S NAME
       ADDRESS

Dated _____   Your Name,
                                              Defendant

****

Send the original and two copies of the two documents to the court and a set to the plaintiff with a cover letter as follows:

****

VIA FIRST CLASS AND CERTIFIED MAIL

Date: _____

NAME OF COURT
DIVISION OF COURT
ADDRESS

RE: Docket No. xxxxxxxxxx, Plaintiff's Name vs. Your Name

Dear Sir/Madam:

I am the defendant in the above-entitled action. Enclosed please find the following:

1. Certification Opposing Motion for Summary Judgment

2. Proof of Mailing

Thank you for your kind attention and cooperation

Sincerely,

Signature
NAME xxxxxxx, Defendant
ADDRESS
CITY, STATE, ZIP
EMAILADDRESS: xxxxxx
PHONE NO.

****

If you send your opposition to the court on time, it is very unlikely for the court to grant the plaintiff's motion for summary judgment. It is possible for the court to schedule a hearing. If the plaintiff attends the hearing, you can demand to see the documents listed on your Request for Production of Documents. If he cannot produce them, you can move for dismissal with prejudice. If he does not attend the hearing, you can move for dismissal with prejudice. If for some reason something went wrong somewhere and the plaintiff is granted a judgment against you, there is still hope, by filing a motion to vacate judgment. We will discuss this and other important court forms in Volume 3 of this series.

You can file your own motion, **Defendant's Motion for Summary Judgment.** Check with your county court clerk or in the law section of the public library for your state's standard **"Motion for Summary Judgment"** form. Different states have different forms and requirements. Some states require a **"Proposed Order Granting Summary Judgment"**. The most important point is to define your reasons for your motion. In the pleading section just type:

"Defendant, (Your Name) respectfully moves for summary judgment.

- The plaintiff is in violation of Federal FDCPA Section 809, (15USC 1692g) which says in part "…if the consumer notifies the debt collector in writing within 30 days that the debt, or any portion thereof, is disputed, the debt collector will obtain verification of the debt…and a copy of such verification will be mailed to the consumer by the debt collector…" My request for verification of debt was received by Plaintiff on xxxxxxx and no verification was provided. Plaintiff supplied copies of statements which are insufficient to validate an alleged debt. *In LVNV Funding, L.L.C. v. Colvell, 421 N.J.Super. 1 (App. Div. 2011), the Appellate Division reversed the trial court's grant of summary judgment for the plaintiff because plaintiff failed to submit evidence sufficient to sustain its burden of proof. As with this case, Colvell involved the claim of Plaintiff on an allegedly defaulted credit card account. The opinion of the Court read in part: "In particular, when suing to collect the balance allegedly owed on an unpaid revolving credit card account, the creditor must prove more than merely the total amount remaining unpaid. ...the creditor must set forth the previous balance, and identify all transactions and credits, as well as the periodic rates, the balance on which the finance charge is computed, other charges, if any, the closing date of the billing cycle, and the new balance."*

- Plaintiff failed to prove that a contract exists between Plaintiff and Defendant. In Plaintiff's Response to Defendant's Request for Production of contracts between the parties, Plaintiff replied, "Documents are unavailable" or "to be supplied later". *To prove a contract claim, Plaintiff must provide proof of an offer, acceptance, consideration, breach and causally related damages, Weichert Realtors v. Ryan, 128 N.J. 427, 435 (1992). Here the contract must be in writing. The Truth in Lending Act at 15 U.S.C. § 1637(a) requires the essential terms of a credit card account be disclosed in writing. In addition, creditors are required to post on the internet the written agreement between the creditor and the consumer for each credit card account under an open-ended consumer credit plan, 15 U.S.C. § 1632(d)(1). Plaintiff cannot prove the basis for any finance or interest charges, late fees and other charges, payment due dates, or even whether Defendant breached an obligation, without a contract. Consequently, someone with the requisite personal knowledge must be able to identify the controlling contract and, in the absence of Defendant's signature, demonstrate what conduct evidences mutual assent to the purported terms. Turning to breach and damages, Plaintiff must have a competent witness who can establish that each charge was authorized because the Truth in Lending Act imposes that burden on Plaintiff. 15 U.S.C. § 1643(b). As Plaintiff bears the burden of proof, absent such proof, Defendant's right to summary judgment should be recognized. That right can only be defeated by Plaintiff's submission of admissible evidence to establish every element of its cause of action. See, James Talcott, Inc. v. Shulman, 82 N.J. Super 438, 443 (App. Div. 1964); see also Robbins v. Jersey City, 23 N.J. 229, 241 (1957); cf., Colvell, supra (debt buyer's summary judgment motion rejected because it failed to submit sufficient admissible evidence to establish its claim based on a purchased credit card account). The standards particularly significant to what evidence Plaintiff must submit are the business records exception, Evid.R. 803(c)(6), the requirement for a witness's personal knowledge, Evid.R. 602, proper authentication of documents, Evid.R. 901 and Evid.R. 902, and submission of originals, Evid.R. 1002. Read together, these rules require that:*

1) Plaintiff produce competent witnesses with sufficient personal knowledge to authenticate and lay the proper foundation for the admission of hearsay materials, and 2) The admissible records be sufficient to carry Plaintiff's evidentiary burden. Presumably, proof of information about the alleged account derives from electronically stored records. In Hahnemann University Hosp. v. Dudnick, 292 N.J.Super. 11, 18 (App. Div. 1996), the Appellate Division held: A witness is competent to lay the foundation for systematically prepared computer records if the witness (1) can demonstrate that the computer record is what the proponent claims and (2) is sufficiently familiar with the record system used and (3) can establish that it was the regular practice of that business to make the record. Consequently, "[a]ttorney affidavits or certifications that are not based on personal knowledge constitute objectionable hearsay." Higgins v. Thurber, 413 N.J. Super. 1, 21 n.19 (App. Div. 2010), aff'd, 205 N.J. 227 (2011) citing Gonzalez v. Ideal Tile Importing Co., Inc., 371 N.J. Super. 349, 358, aff'd, 184 N.J. 415 (2005) ("Even an attorney's sworn statement will have no bearing when the attorney has no personal knowledge of the facts asserted"); see, also, Wells Fargo Bank, N.A. v. Ford, 418 N.J.Super. 592, 599 (App. Div. 2011). It is difficult to imagine in a case such as this one – which involves an allegedly defaulted credit card account assigned by the original creditor – that there would be anyone with personal knowledge of the elements of Plaintiff's cause of action. Instead, if the facts can be proven at all, they would need to be through hearsay business records. Thus, it is essential for Plaintiff to submit the affidavits of witnesses who are competent to admit those records and that the proper foundation be laid.

Respectfully, based on the foregoing, Defendant, (Your Name), requests that the Court grant the Motion for Summary Judgment dismissing Plaintiff's Complaint with prejudice.

Dated: _____

_____

Signature
***NAME xxxxxxx*, Pro-se Defendant**
ADDRESS
CITY, STATE, ZIP
***EMAILADDRESS*: xxxxxx**

Collections attorney claims he is not a "debt collector"

One of my readers reported that after filing his own Motion for Summary Judgment, the collections attorney typed his brief in opposition to the motion with the following (Point 1) argument:

****

"The Plaintiff is not a "Debt Collector" as defined by 15 USC 1692a and therefore cannot be in violation of the Fair Debt Collections Practices Act (FDCPA). All claims in this motion address the actions of the Plaintiff's (bank/cc Company) attorneys. The term "debt collector" does not include "any officer or a creditor while, in the name of the creditor, collecting debts for such creditor". 15USC 1692a further states:

The term "creditor" means any person who offers or extends credit creating a debt or to whom a debt is owed, but such term does not include any person to the extent that he receives an assignment or transfer of a debt in default solely for the purpose of facilitating collection of such debt for another.

Therefore, the Plaintiff (bank/cc Company), being the original creditor, is not a debt collector. There was no assignment or transfer of the debt which would create a debt collector in another entity". – end of brief

****

The foregoing argument appears to be a desperate move by the plaintiff's attorney who is either confused or is deliberately trying to confuse the defendant in this case. As a rebuttal to Plaintiff's Point 1, the defendant submitted the following:

DEFENDANT'S REBUTTAL TO POINT 1:

Attorney for Plaintiff alleges that Plaintiff and its collection attorney are EXEMPT from FDCPA rules because Plaintiff and its attorney are NOT debt collectors. Plaintiff's attorney pasted the following excerpt from FDCPA USC 15, 1692a (4),

"The term "creditor" means any person who offers or extends credit creating a debt or to whom a debt is owed, but such term does not include any person to the extent that he receives an assignment or transfer of a debt in default solely for the purpose of facilitating collection of such debt for another."

The above excerpt from this subchapter defines a creditor NOT a collector. Plaintiff and its collection attorney are in fact debt collectors pursuant to the same section as defined below:

*6) The term "debt collector" means any person who uses any instrumentality of interstate commerce or the mails in any business the principal purpose of which is the collection of any debts, or who regularly collects or attempts to collect, directly or indirectly, debts owed or due or asserted to be owed or due another. Notwithstanding the exclusion provided by clause (F) of the last sentence of this paragraph, **the term includes any creditor** who, in the process of collecting his own debts, uses any name other than his own which would indicate that a third person is collecting or attempting to collect such debts. For the purpose of section 1692f(6) of this title, such term also includes any person who uses any instrumentality of interstate commerce or the mails in any business the principal purpose of which is the enforcement of security interests. The term does not include --*

(A) any officer or employee of a creditor while, in the name of the creditor, collecting debts for such creditor;

(B) any person while acting as a debt collector for another person, both of whom are related by common ownership or affiliated by corporate control, if the person acting as a debt collector does so only for persons to whom it is so related or affiliated and if the principal business of such person is not the collection of debts;

(C) any officer or employee of the United States or any State to the extent that collecting or attempting to collect any debt is in the performance of his official duties;

(D) any person while serving or attempting to serve legal process on any other person in connection with the judicial enforcement of any debt;

(E) any nonprofit organization which, at the request of consumers, performs bona fide consumer credit counseling and assists consumers in the liquidation of their debts by receiving payments from such consumers and distributing such amounts to creditors; and

(F) any person collecting or attempting to collect any debt owed or due or asserted to be owed or due another to the extent such activity (i) is incidental to a bona fide fiduciary obligation or a bona fide escrow arrangement; (ii) concerns a debt which was originated by such person; (iii) concerns a debt which was not in default at the time it was obtained by such person; or (iv) concerns a debt obtained by such person as a secured party in a commercial credit transaction involving the creditor.

It is clear from the above section that the Plaintiff's attorney is a collector and is NOT EXEMPT from the FDCPA rules. Finally, as further proof the Plaintiff's attorney is a debt collector and thereby subject to the FDCPA rules, I hereby enclose collection letters from the attorney whereby the last sentence on the bottom of each letter states, **"This communication is from a debt collector and any information obtained will be used for that purpose"**.

After the reader sent the above rebuttal to the court, the attorney stopped communicating. However, the Court still scheduled a hearing. The reader reported to me that the Plaintiff's attorney did not show up in Court. The judge tried to contact him by phone when the docket was called. When the plaintiff's attorney did not answer, the judge dismissed the case with prejudice. ". – end of rebuttal

****

Do you have to pay tax on the cancelled debt?

It depends. In my case, the credit card companies sent me forms 1099-C (CODI-Cancellation of Debt Income) for the supposed cancelled debt, not in the year the debt was cancelled but after another year has passed. It put me in a terrible position of having unexpected income in the wrong year. To make matters worse, I filed taxes for the designated year before receiving the forms 1099-C. I set aside the problem until I received an IRS tax deficiency assessment letter claiming that I have an underpayment of $22,500. So I had to do some legal and taxation research, then sent the IRS the following reply:

****

By FIRST CLASS AND CERTIFIED MAIL RETURN RECEIPT REQUESTED
Date: _____
IRS OFFICE
ADDRESS
    RE: SS# _____,   Letter #_____

Dear Sir or Madam (it is better to address your letter to the IRS agent who sent you the letter):

I am in receipt of your letter a copy of which is enclosed indicating a tax deficiency of $22,500. Please be informed that I am disputing this amount for the following reasons:

-The creditors were unable to validate my alleged debt. Creditors could not ascertain if I am in fact the debtor. See attached copies of my letters for Validation of Debt, attached herewith as Exhibits A and B for which no reply was received. If the creditors can provide the proof requested on the enclosed letters, then the alleged cancelled debt shown on Form 1099-C is correct and taxable.

- U.S. Code – Title 26 Section 6201(d), states:
(d) Required reasonable verification of information returns- In any court proceeding, if a taxpayer asserts a reasonable dispute with respect to any item of income reported on an information return filed with the Secretary under subpart B or C of part III of subchapter A of chapter 61 by a third party and the taxpayer has fully cooperated with the Secretary (including providing, within a reasonable period of time, access to and inspection of all witnesses, information, and documents within the control of the taxpayer as reasonably requested by the Secretary), the Secretary shall have the burden of producing reasonable and probative information concerning such deficiency in addition to such information return.

    Pursuant to the above section, please direct the creditors to provide positive proof that I am in fact the debtor for the cancelled debt shown on the enclosed copies of 1099-C. Positive acceptable proof are copies of my signed application for credit showing my social security number and signed credit card charges equaling the amount shown on the 1099-C.

Respectfully,
Your Name
Address
Email Address:
Phone No.

****

    As stated in Section 6201(d), the IRS has the burden of proof when you dispute the amounts on Forms 1099-C. They must obtain verification from the issuer of the 1099-C that the person they issued the form to is in fact the correct person.

    I never heard back from the IRS after sending this letter. It has been over 7 years so I assume they were unable to obtain the proof from the creditors. There are other ways to deal with

IRS Form 1099-C such as filing an IRS Form 8275, Disclosure Statement or proving to the IRS that you were insolvent at the time of cancellation of your debt. Insolvency simply means your liabilities exceed your assets. For starters, you must fill out IRS Form 982, a worksheet to calculate your cancellation of debt income (CODI). This will be discussed in more detail in Volume 3 of this series.

If your debt was discharged through bankruptcy, the creditor is not supposed to report the amount to the IRS on Form 1099-C. It is not considered income and therefore not taxable. Your creditors should receive notice of discharge of your debt through bankruptcy and should not send you a 1099-C, but some creditors may still ignore the notices and send out a 1099-C anyway. You simply need to complete IRS Form 982, and attach it to your tax return to provide notice to the IRS that the debt was discharged in bankruptcy and the discharged amount will not be included as income.

If the IRS is able to obtain verification pursuant to U.S. Code – Title 26 Section 6201(d) and you were not insolvent, you will have to pay tax on the cancelled debt. However, make sure that the proof the IRS receives from the issuer includes your credit card application showing your signature and correct SS number. This is the only positive proof that the cancelled debt really belongs to you. A generic unsigned Cardmember agreement won't do. In the absence of any positive proof, write the IRS again to point out that your SSN cannot be associated with the cancelled debt.

How to Mitigate Negative Credit Report

After I settled my 4 credit card balances for an average of 10% of my total debt and obtained a judgment with prejudice against the 5th creditor that sued me, I was finally "credit card debt free". Shortly thereafter, it so happened that mortgage interest rates came down drastically and we wanted to refinance. The monthly mortgage payment on a $350,000 mortgage loan at 7% APR is substantially higher than a loan at 4.5% APR which was the prevailing mortgage rate at that time. We filled out the application for refinance anyway just to give it a try knowing that "something" negative would probably show up on account of all the forgiven debt. Sure enough the mortgage underwriter called me within a day of submitting the application to inform me that my FICO scores were very low, at 580 if you average my scores at all the three major reporting agencies. He then emailed me my credit reports and highlighted all the negative information. The negative information were the credit card balances that were written off and which show up on the credit reports as "Charge Off". I told the underwriter that 4 of them were paid in accordance with settlement agreements and the 5th one failed to validate my debt in accordance with FDCPA, then sent him a copy of judgment from the court. He typed up a sworn statement (a.k.a. Certification or Affidavit) indicating the 4 accounts were "paid as agreed" and the 5th was an invalidated debt. I signed the statement in front of a notary public. Then the underwriter approved my refinance application for 4.5% APR. End of the story, right? NO. Before he shook my hand to close the deal, he gave me a parting advice that I should write to the creditors and major reporting agencies to dispute the negative information. I did just that and wrote the following letter to the credit card companies:

****

Dear Credit Card Company:

I am disputing your report to XYZ Reporting Agency that the balance on my account was a "Charge Off". Please correct your report to indicate that the balance was "Paid as Agreed". There was a mutual agreement between both parties of the settlement amount.

****

I received basically the same reply as shown below from all the credit card companies:

Dear Debtor:

According to the rules of Fair Credit Reporting Act, the negative information must stay on your account for 7 years.

****

I must admit that after receiving the above letter, I was ready to give up. I was not planning to apply for any other loans in the near future, but I wanted to see how far I could take it and I had a little bit of time in my hands. So I wrote a follow up letter to each of them and when I received no reply, I called the county court clerk for instructions on filing Small Claims against each one of them. She directed me to the website where I found a fillable small claims form and instructions Most court clerks should be able to provide a small claims form. After fiddling with the form for a while, I finally came up with the finished product which approximates the small claims Complaint shown below. Please be reminded that the names that were used are fictitious and were used only for illustration:

****

Plaintiff's Information:
Name: (Your Name)
Address:
Phone:

YOUR NAME

Plaintiff

v.

WASHINGTON MUTUAL BANK
Alan Fishman, CEO
John Maciel, CFO
Jezel Krupak, Secretary

Defendant

SMALL CLAIMS COURT

COMPLAINT FOR DAMAGES

Defendant Information:
Name: **Washington Mutual - Short Hills**
Address:
Phone:

Plaintiff, by way of Complaint says:

Defendants are in violation of the following laws:

- Fair Credit Reporting Act
- Fair Debt Collection Practices Act
- Defamation of Character

Defendants reported erroneous negative information on my credit reports and refused to make the necessary correction, see my enclosed letter requesting Defendant to make correction.

Defendants reported my credit card account as "Charge Off" although they agreed to accept a settlement of the balance for a mutually agreed amount.

Therefore, the report must be corrected from "Charge Off" to, "Paid as agreed".

Wherefore, plaintiff requests judgment against defendants for damages in the amount of $3000, together with attorney's fees, if applicable, costs of suit, and any other relief as the court may deem proper.

by: _____
Your Name, Defendant Pro-se

Dated:

****

I mailed the summons and Complaints by certified mail to the credit card companies. I wanted to wait for the green postal proof of receipt so I may file the Complaint with the Court but much to my very pleasant surprise attorneys of the credit card companies (Banks) called me to let me know they wanted to settle the lawsuit by correcting the information on my credit reports. Two of them asked if I had already filed the suits. They wanted to reimburse me for the Court fees and they even drafted a Stipulation of Settlement. Fortunately, I had not sent the papers to the Court yet. When it became clear to me that I've gained the upper hand, for a moment I wanted to act like a scoundrel and demand $2000 from each of them for violating my rights but I controlled myself and agreed to the settlement they proposed, i.e. to change my credit records for the cancelled debt from "Charge Off" to "Paid as Agreed".

    The observative reader will notice that I have included the names of bank officers as co-Defendants in the lawsuit. This is a trick that in my experience has always worked. If you are suing someone or if you are filing a counter-suit, include the highest ranking officers of your adversary as opposing parties in your claim. The bank officers are probably pulling in millions of dollars a year in salaries and bonuses. Their time is gold and do not want to be bothered by small nuisance claims such as yours. The likelihood is they will direct the responsible employee in their company to quickly settle the suit just like what happened in my case.

5 Smart Ways to Improve Your Credit

1. Keep your balances low. If they are high, pay them down.
2. Pay off small card balances, then use one or two cards for everything.
3. Don't get rid of old credit card accounts. They help show a solid repayment history.
4. Pay your bills on time. A large number of late bills can impact your credit score.
5. Review your credit report and communicate any problems you see to the 3 major credit bureaus, Experian, TransUnion and Equifax. File small claims suits against the creditor and reporting agencies who refuse to make the necessary correction for violation of the Fair Credit Reporting Act, (FCRA), 15 U.S.C. § 1681 et seq. https://www.consumer.ftc.gov/sites/default/files/articles/pdf/pdf-0111-fair-credit-reporting-act.pdf

See previous topic, "How to Mitigate Negative Credit Report. Also visit my website: www.Arthur V. Prosper.com for additional information.

Factors That Affect Credit Scores

The tables below will give the reader an idea of how the credit reporting agencies calculate your credit scores.

% Of Payments Made On Time
35% IMPACT ON SCORE
- BELOW AVG

0% - 1%

- AVERAGE

2% - 59%

- GOOD

60% - 89%

- EXCELLENT

90% - 100%

Why does payment history matter? A history of late payments makes lenders question whether you'll make future payments on time. A payment that is late by 30 days or more is often reported to the credit bureaus. Credit Tip: Set up autopay or bill pay reminders so you receive email or text messages reminding you when bills are due. How I compare to others.
- 12%

Below Avg
- 17%

Average
- 9%

Good
- 61%

Excellent

****

Age of Your Oldest Account
15% IMPACT ON SCORE

- **BELOW AVG**
  Less than 2 years

- **AVERAGE**
  2 - 7 years

- **GOOD**
  8 - 25 years

- **EXCELLENT**
  More than 25 years

Why does the age of your accounts matter? The age of your oldest credit account shows lenders how much experience you have handling credit, hinting at your overall reliability.

Credit Tip: Keep your oldest accounts open and in good standing to lengthen your credit history and help your score.

How I compare to others.

- 5%
  Below Avg
- 18%
  Average
- 56%
  Good
- 21%
  Excellent

****

% Of Credit Used
30% IMPACT ON SCORE

- BELOW AVG
More than 60%

- AVERAGE
30% - 59%

- GOOD
10% - 29%

- EXCELLENT – Less than 10%

Why does how much credit you're using matter? Lenders look for signs of responsible credit usage, and the better you are at living within your means, the better it is for your score. If you are using most of your credit, it may be difficult for you to get additional credit or credit with a good interest rate. Credit Tip: Using less than 30% of your available credit is a good goal, but keep in mind that using some available credit and paying it off monthly may be better than not using any credit at all. How I compare to others.

- 20%
Below Avg
- 15%
Average
- 20%
Good
- 45%
Excellent

****

Inquiries Made In the Past 2 Years
5% IMPACT ON SCORE

- BELOW AVG
  More than 5

- AVERAGE
  3 - 5

- GOOD
  1 - 2

- EXCELLENT - None

Why do recent inquiries matter? Lenders tend to see too many recent inquiries for your credit score as a sign of risk. Most lenders are lenient when they see similar inquiries reported close together because they understand you are shopping around for the lowest rate. Credit Tip: Since lenders are only considering inquiries for the past two years, try to spread out when you borrow money or get new credit cards by a few years. How I compare to others.

- 10%
  Below Avg
- 17%
  Average
- 31%
  Good
- 42%
  Excellent

****

Accounts Opened In the Past 2 Years
10% IMPACT ON SCORE
- BELOW AVG

More than 6

- AVERAGE
  5 - 6

- GOOD
  3 - 4

- EXCELLENT
  Less than 3

Why does opening new accounts matter? From a lender's perspective, opening too many new accounts in a short window of time could point to credit problems. Credit Tip: Try to limit the number of credit accounts you have, and if possible, wait a few years between opening new accounts. How I compare to others.

- 4%
Below Avg
- 6%
Average
- 15%
Good
- 76%
Excellent

****

Total Available Credit
5% IMPACT ON SCORE
- BELOW AVG
Less than $2.5K

- AVERAGE
  $2.5K - $15K

- GOOD
  $15K - $50K

- EXCELLENT
  More than $50K

Why does available credit matter? Plenty of available credit, compared to the amount owed shows lenders that you're managing credit responsibly. Credit Tip: Don't borrow more than you need without fully paying off other loans. And, be sure to keep your credit card balances under 30 % -35 % of your available credit line. How I compare to others.

- 28%
  Below Avg
- 28%
  Average
- 32%
  Good
- 12%
  Excellent

****

The bank can freeze your checking and savings accounts

While you are in the middle of negotiating forgiveness for your credit card debts, there is a chance that the bank will deduct money from your own or your spouse's checking or savings account and explain it as a "Bad Debt Recovery Offset" in states that allow creditors to do this. Normally, the bank thinks it has the right to do this if any of the following is true:
- You were a co-signor on your spouse's credit card
- You guaranteed each other's debts
- There was something in your cc agreement that they think gives them the right to recover unpaid balances from your bank accounts.
- The bank that issued your credit card is using "Common Law Right to Setoff" which is in the agreement you and your spouse signed.
- The cc company won a default judgment against you without your knowledge and has put a lien on your bank account.

To prevent this from happening, withdraw your money and close your account at a bank that issued your credit card. Better still, to play it safe, withdraw your money and your spouse's money from all banking institutions and pay for everything in cash or money order or ask a relative to issue checks on your behalf and reimburse them. I know this is extremely inconvenient but unfortunately this is a sacrifice you have to bear until your credit card debts are forgiven or written off. Google: "debtor friendly states" to read various articles that may provide information on whether or not creditors have the right in your particular state to freeze your bank accounts, put a lien on your properties and/or garnish your wages.

What really happens after creditor files suit?

The creditor's objective in collections is to collect the maximum amount they can collect from a debtor while expending as little effort, energy and time as possible. Your objective as a debtor is to convince the creditor that it is in their best interest to accept the amount you say you can afford to pay as full settlement of your account. These opposing objectives equally apply before and after the creditor files a lawsuit. To summarize, these are the steps your creditor is likely to take after filing suit and what you should do in response:

1) You receive a summons from the court attached to the Creditor's Complaint. The creditor is hoping that you will either fail to answer the complaint in which case he can move for entry of a default judgment against you or that you will call them to negotiate a settlement. In most states, if a creditor wins a default judgment, your wages may be garnished and/or a lien may be filed on your properties and/or your bank accounts may be frozen.

- Your Response: You will reply to the Complaint within the time indicated on the summons. See Chapter, Creditor/Plaintiff's Complaint for a sample reply. With your answer, you will also include Defendant Discoveries, i.e. a "Request for Admissions", "Interrogatories" and a "Request for Production of Documents". You may or may not include a "Motion for Summary Judgment". See samples of these legal documents in Volume 3.

2) When the creditor receives these legal documents, they will either, A) call you to negotiate a settlement. They will be more likely to settle for a lesser amount after receiving your legal documents, or B) They will reply to your Discoveries with "copy and paste" canned Answers produced by an office clerk. In all likelihood, an attorney will not even have time

to review the canned Answers. They may reply to your Request for Production of Documents by indicating one or more of the documents you have requested are "unavailable" or "to be supplied later". They may reply to your Request for Admissions and Interrogatories with a combination of these answers: "Objection, irrelevant, compound, frivolous, vague, uses terms not defined, calls for a legal conclusion, subject to attorney-client privilege, overbroad, burdensome, not tailored to lead to discovery of admissible evidence. They may oppose your Motion for Summary Judgment by citing court cases to offer precedence for their legal arguments.

- Your Response: A) If they call to settle, do not say much. Tell them to put their settlement offer in writing. At this point, it becomes a negotiation which may be expedited by email. So do not hesitate to give them your email address. Communicate in writing rather than discuss the matter by phone. Negotiate the offer down to between 5% and 15% of the amount they sued for. See Volume 3, Rejection of Settlement Offer. If you come to an agreement, get a release from them and a stipulation for dismissal of the case. B) If they reply to your Discoveries, immediately write the court for adjournment of the hearing if it has been scheduled. In general, in most jurisdictions, the judge would allow at least 1 adjournment for each opposing party. See Chapter 3/Letters, "Second Request for Adjournment". A court appearance will put you at a disadvantage because the lawyer is more familiar with court proceedings. It's a given. He has spent more time in court than you. Even though the law may be in your favor due to the fact that the lawyer has no evidence to sustain the Plaintiff's burden of proof, if you both appear for the hearing, he will surely take advantage of you. Heck, even he himself does not know if you really owe the money. His client, the CC Company just told him you do, which is hearsay. When your case is called, he will pull you aside in one of the hallways and try to intimidate you by saying, "Let's get real. You know you owe the money. Why don't we stop wasting each other's time and just tell me how much you can afford to pay each month". In some jurisdictions, you will be compelled to try to settle in front of a mediator first. This procedure usually lightens the load for the judge since the majority of the cases are settled through mediation. The attorney will prefer a mediator to a judge. The judge will surely ask him why he cannot produce any evidence for his allegations. But the mediator will not. His job is to get the case settled. He will be more focused in trying to work out a compromise between the parties. In my own experience, the mediators I've encountered were not lawyers but court clerks, volunteers, paralegals and law school students who knew very little about the law but had more respect for a lawyer than me. I've fared better in front of judges than in front of mediators. The mediator more than likely will have more of an affinity for the attorney than you who might be painted outright as a deadbeat by the attorney. Oftentimes, if the lawyer outright does not like you, he will try to scare you by saying he will pursue perjury charges against you if you do not admit to the debt. For one of my readers who related his experience to me, this was how the conversation went when the collection attorney pulled him aside in the court's hallway to talk to him:

- Plaintiff's Attorney ("PA"): So you're having financial difficulties?
- Defendant/Credit Card Holder ("D"): Keeps his mouth shut, does not reply.
- PA: So when do you think you can pay this balance (PA shows him a statement)?
- D: You filed the Complaint (trying to say as little as possible)
- PA: Are you denying you owe this money? Isn't this credit card account yours?
- D: Did you bring proof that it's mine?

- PA: Let's stop playing games. How much can you pay right now so we can go home? We both know this is your account.
- D: Do you know if this is my account? Where is your proof?
- PA: The bank has been sending you statements which you have been receiving at this address. This is your address isn't it?
- D: Yes it is. Do you have proof of mailing? Do you have proof that I received any of the statements?
- PA: Oh c'mon let's stop playing games. You have been paying these statements all along then suddenly you stopped paying. Maybe you are going through some tough times. The bank can understand that. Why don't you tell me how much you can pay today? If you cannot pay anything today, maybe we can set up a monthly installment. Will that work for you, so we can go home?
- D: But you have no proof that I owe any money. Even you don't know if I owe any money at all. How will you prove to the judge that I owe money if you have no proof?
- PA: Listen. I've had it. If we go in front of the judge and I ask you if this is your account and you lie, I'll charge you with perjury. You know what that means doncha? It's a felony you know, and you can go to jail.
- D: Yeah, yeah. But I will not lie. All I'll tell him is that the burden of proof is on you to produce evidence for your Complaint. Even you don't know if I even owe a penny. Your client told you so. It's hearsay. You wanna try the case? Go ahead…all the way the Supreme Court if you want. Just come up with the evidence.
- PA: Alright, I don't really have time for this. If I give you a discount of 50% of the balance, can you afford to pay that, even in installments?

TO MAKE A LONG STORY SHORT, it became a negotiation after that. From my books, he felt empowered to engage the PA in a spirited discussion. But at that point, he was given 3 courses of action, 1) to stay and continue to negotiate with the PA, 2) tell the PA that he wants the judge to hear the case, 3) tell the PA to shove it and just walk out of the court and in so doing, the PA may just walk out too, or the PA may wait for the judge or mediator and explain that he discussed the case with the Defendant and was not able to come up with an agreement. It is unlikely that he will move for a judgment against Defendant at this point because the Defendant made a personal appearance which was recorded by the court clerk. As it turned out, my reader opted for choice no. 1 and negotiated a 15% final settlement of the account with the PA.

****

Although the above experience turned out well for this particular reader since he was able to negotiate down his balance to 15%, going to court is very stressful for most people. Therefore, you should try to avoid a court appearance in any way possible. Write the court the following letter as soon as you receive the Plaintiff's reply to your Discoveries:

****

RE: Docket No._____, Plaintiff's Name vs. Your Name

Dear Hon. Presiding Judge:

I am the defendant in the above entitled case. With this letter I am requesting adjournment of this case until such time that plaintiff is able to produce the documents requested in my Discoveries, particularly my First Request for Production of Documents dated _____. The Plaintiff received my Discoveries on _____ as shown on the enclosed copy of USPS postal receipt. As shown on the enclosed Plaintiff's Answers, The Plaintiff's answers to Requests 1, 2 and 3 are "unavailable" and/or "to be supplied later". Title 15 U.S. Code § 1643(b) requires Plaintiff/card issuer to provide proof as stated below:

15 U.S. Code § 1643(b) - Liability of holder of credit card
(b) Burden of proof

In any action by a card issuer to enforce liability for the use of a credit card, the burden of proof is upon the card issuer to show that the use was authorized or, if the use was unauthorized, then the burden of proof is upon the card issuer to show that the conditions of liability for the unauthorized use of a credit card, as set forth in subsection (a), have been met. Respectfully, as a matter of law, the Plaintiff must comply with the foregoing Title and Section. Wherefore, defendant prays that an indefinite adjournment be granted until such time that Plaintiff is able to satisfy the burden of proof requirement as to its allegations.

Sincerely,

Signature
NAME xxxxxxxx, Pro-se Defendant
ADDRESS
CITY, STATE, ZIP
EMAILADDRESS: xxxxxx
Tel# xxxxxxxx
Email Address: xxxxxxxxx

Cc: Plaintiff
****

      In my experience with two prior cases, after I've sent the above-mentioned letter requesting the court for an adjournment, the court granted the adjournment and then I never heard from the plaintiff's attorney again. **Another recent case reported by a reader:** The court rejected his request and ordered both parties for a hearing. He was not a fighter so when both parties appeared in court, in front of a mediator, the attorney scared him into admitting to his debt and persuaded him that paying 50% of the amount of the suit was "a deal made in heaven" for him. Still better than paying 100% plus legal fees. The attorney made the deal probably because he is aware that he could not sustain the burden of proof if the case had gone to trial. If you are a fighter and firmly believe that the law is on your side (as I do), do not let the attorney intimidate you when you see each other in court. This is their game. Don't fall for it. When he pulls you aside, do not give in whatever he says. Just say you want the judge to hear the case. If he asks you to go with him inside one of the rooms with a mediator, tell him you want the judge to hear the case not a mediator. Unless the amount being demanded is huge, say more than $50,000, there is a 90% chance that the attorney will come to his senses and may ask, "What is your best offer for a settlement?" Tell him 5%. Go up to 15% if you think you can scrounge up enough cash.

    The purpose of the hearing (Pre-Trial Conference) is for the judge to determine if there should be a full trial. The judge will issue an opinion after the hearing. In the hearing, the attorney for the plaintiff will give his argument verbally and show the judge copies of your credit card statements and letters from you. This will be all the evidence he will bring to court based on his answers to your Request for Production of Documents. When the judge calls you to present your side, you can recite the following:

- Your honor, the burden of proof is on the plaintiff to prove his allegations. And this is based on law, **Title 15 U.S. Code § 1643(b) - Liability of holder of credit card.**
- The plaintiff is in violation of **The Federal FDCPA Section 809, (15USC 1692g)** which says in part "…if the consumer notifies the debt collector in writing within 30 days that the debt, or any portion thereof, is disputed, the debt collector will obtain verification of the debt…and a copy of such verification will be mailed to the consumer by the debt collector..." My request for verification of debt was received by Plaintiff on xxxxxxx and no verification was provided. Plaintiff supplied copies of statements which are insufficient to validate an alleged debt. In LVNV Funding, L.L.C. v. Colvell, 421

N.J.Super. 1 (App. Div. 2011), the Appellate Division reversed the trial court's grant of summary judgment for the plaintiff because plaintiff failed to submit evidence sufficient to sustain its burden of proof. As with this case, Colvell involved the claim of Plaintiff on an allegedly defaulted credit card account. The opinion of the Court read in part: "In particular, when suing to collect the balance allegedly owed on an unpaid revolving credit card account, the creditor must prove more than merely the total amount remaining unpaid. ...the creditor must set forth the previous balance, and identify all transactions and credits, as well as the periodic rates, the balance on which the finance charge is computed, other charges, if any, the closing date of the billing cycle, and the new balance."

- Plaintiff failed to prove that a contract exists between Plaintiff and Defendant. In Plaintiff's Response to Defendant's Request for Production of contracts between the parties, Plaintiff replied, "Documents are unavailable". To prove a contract claim, Plaintiff must provide proof of an offer, acceptance, consideration, breach and causally related damages. Weichert Realtors v. Ryan, 128 N.J. 427, 435 (1992). Here, the contract must be in writing. The Truth in Lending Act at 15 U.S.C. § 1637(a) requires the essential terms of a credit card account be disclosed in writing. In addition, creditors are required to post on the internet the written agreement between the creditor and the consumer for each credit card account under an open-ended consumer credit plan, 15 U.S.C. § 1632(d)(1). Plaintiff cannot prove the basis for any finance or interest charges, late fees and other charges, payment due dates, or even whether Defendant breached an obligation, without a contract. Consequently, someone with the requisite personal knowledge must be able to identify the controlling contract and, in the

absence of Defendant's signature, demonstrate what conduct evidences mutual assent to the purported terms. Turning to breach and damages, Plaintiff must have a competent witness who can establish that each charge was authorized because the Truth in Lending Act imposes that burden on Plaintiff. 15 U.S.C. § 1643(b).
- As Plaintiff bears the burden of proof, absent such proof, Defendant's right to summary judgment should be recognized. That right can only be defeated by Plaintiff's submission of admissible evidence to establish every element of its cause of action. See, James Talcott, Inc. v. Shulman, 82 N.J. Super 438, 443 (App. Div. 1964); see also Robbins v. Jersey City, 23 N.J. 229, 241 (1957); cf., Colvell, supra (debt buyer's summary judgment motion rejected because it failed to submit sufficient admissible evidence to establish its claim based on a purchased credit card account). The standards particularly significant to what evidence Plaintiff must submit are the business records exception, Evid.R. 803(c)(6), the requirement for a witness's personal knowledge, Evid.R. 602, proper authentication of documents, Evid.R. 901 and Evid.R. 902, and submission of originals, Evid.R. 1002.
- Your honor, with respect, even the attorney for the Plaintiff has no idea whether or not the statements of account which he entered into evidence are accurate or if they even belong to me. Based on this, your honor, I move for a Motion Dismissing this case with prejudice.

After giving your testimony, the judge may give the attorney a chance to cross-examine you (ask you questions). When it happened to me, this is the way the cross-examination went:

Plaintiff's Attorney (PA): Do you have a credit card account with MBNA?
Me: I object to the question. The burden of proof is on you to prove that. You filed the Complaint
PA: Did you open an account with MBNA?

Me: I object to the question. The burden of proof is on you to prove that. You filed the Complaint

PA: Did you use MBNA's credit card to purchase goods?

Me: I object to the question. The burden of proof is on you to prove that. You filed the Complaint

Some of my readers have reported that they have learned a lot from this book and have used the same tactics I've used to their advantage, to beat back the plaintiff's attorney in a hearing. The following is an example of a reader's exchange with the plaintiff's attorney:

PA: Is this debt yours?

Defendant: Please let me see the statements. Do you have any invoices or charge slips that make up this total amount (pointing to the balance on the statement)? Do you have a detailed amortization schedule of the daily interest charges? Do you have proof that I agreed to the interest charges?

PA: When you used your credit card, you agreed to all the interest charges and agreed to be bound by the rules and regulations of MBNA.

Defendant: Is there anything in the law that states, if I use my credit card that "I agreed to be bound by the rules and regulations of MBNA? Do you have a signed agreement from me?"

PA: What is your occupation and what are your monthly wages?

Defendant: I object to the question which is irrelevant and inappropriate. You have not won a judgment against me. My income and assets are not relevant at this time.

PA: How much can you pay so that we can make this go away so that we won't be wasting the precious time of this court?

Defendant: The burden of proof is on you, the plaintiff. You have not proven that I owe any amount. You yourself do not even know if the MBNA statements are correct. You are in violation of the FDCPA rules.

Conclusion – Volume 2

Volume 1 provided the reader with the strategy for negotiating credit card debt down to 5% and gave the reader a better understanding of the actions and reactions of the creditors, collectors and attorneys involved in the collection process. This volume provides the necessary tools in dealing with the negotiation-resistant creditor and to use the system legally to obtain debt forgiveness. This book contains a wealth of information obtained from many hours of research and through trial and error. Although there are no guarantees, the methods and strategies discussed in this book worked for me. When I sent my creditors the Validation of Debt letter shown in this book, my creditors were not able to validate my alleged debts. My creditors could not produce the documents requested on my Request for Production of Documents. When I disputed the creditors' Forms 1099-C and requested the IRS to obtain verification of debt from the creditors in accordance with U.S. Code – Title 26 Section 6201(d), I never heard from the IRS again.

After my debts were forgiven, the nightmare was over so I was able to start my life anew, free from credit card debt. I was able to focus on taking care of my family. I kept 2 credit cards and continued to use them. They carried small credit lines, one for $7,000 and the other for $5,000. I pay the balances of the accounts as soon as I receive the monthly statements. My FICO credit scores initially took a dive to the high 500s but after only 7 years, I am back to the high 700s and even got to 800 for a few months last year. I started receiving pre-approved credit card offers again in the mail a few years ago. I feel really blessed that I did not have to file for bankruptcy and that the path I took enabled me to write this book which I hope will help a lot of people, who are in the same predicament as I was, to accomplish the same thing I've accomplished---a credit card debt free life.

*****End of Volume 2*****

The Simplest Path to Wealth: Turn $50,000 into $3.3 Million

If you have a tax deferred retirement plan, an IRA, a 401k, 403b or 457b and your money is invested in the stock market, are you prepared to lose 30 to 60% of your money when the market crashes? It is not a question of "if" but "when". It is guaranteed the stock market will crash when the next recession arrives, but when will that be? Learn more. Click on the link below:
The Simplest Path to Wealth: Turn $50,000 into $3.3 Million
https://www.amazon.com/gp/product/B01KPQB0OS/ref=dbs_a_def_rwt_bibl_vppi_i0

Volume 3 Includes:
- What types of assets are judgment proof?
- Repairing your credit
- Motion to dismiss arbitration award - sample
- Interrogatories - sample
- Request for Admissions – sample
- Request for Production of Original Documents - sample
- Motion for Dismissal due to Plaintiff's default - sample
- Motion to Vacate Judgment - sample
- Dispute 1099-C, IRS Form 8275, Disclosure Statement, Insolvency Worksheet
- Statute of Limitation
- Disputing a negative credit report
- How Mediation Works
- Debtor Friendly States
- Letters

****

Learn more about the subjects below from the author's new book:

Living Rich and Loving It:
Your Guide to a Rich, Happy, Healthy, Simple and Balanced Life

https://www.amazon.com/Living-Rich-Loving-healthy-balanced-ebook/dp/B01GORIB4Y/ref=sr_1_3?s=digital-text&ie=UTF8&qid=1471625403&sr=1-3&keywords=Arthur V. Prosper

- o **Find a job you love** – If you cannot wait to get up and get to work every morning, then you have found the job you love. Otherwise, you need to read this chapter and the chapter, "Increase Your Income with these Ideas".

- o **Personal Insurance** – Which is better, whole life or term insurance? How much insurance do you need? The answer may surprise you.

- o **Annuities, what are they?**

- o **Budgeting made easy** - Follow the sample and simple budget in the book and you will always have a monthly surplus.

- o **Never buy Veblen Goods** – the savings will amaze you.

- o **Shop around for everything** – if you are struggling to make ends meet, this chapter will show you why. Learn how to save more and spend less.

- How to purchase your primary residence – Pros and cons of owning vs. renting. The analysis chart shows the clear winner which will surprise you.

- Good debt, bad debt – when borrowing makes sense. Analysis table proves that some debts are good.

- Do Not Take Unnecessary Risks, Don't Do Anything Stupid – this chapter shows that stupidity is the great equalizer in life. Doing any of the things on the list may change your life or worse may end your life in the blink of an eye.

- Never invest in a rental property – this chapter tells you why it is not worth being an absentee landlord.

- Never keep an emergency fund – the analysis chart shows you why and the answer will astound you.

- No Double Taxation on 401k Loans – never ever listen to Suze Orman that 401k loans are taxed twice.

- Planning for College – how to fund your children's college education. Read the many different ideas in this chapter which includes the availability of financial aid packages. The chart shows which colleges to choose and guides you towards a prudent decision.

- Increase Your Income - Make more money in your spare time with these ideas. When you read the money-making ideas in this chapter, you will scratch your head and say, "why didn't I think of that?"

- Create a Document Storage and Retrieval System – So simple yet so effective. It will free up a lot of your limited living space.

- Stress-Free Personal Time Management – This system will organize your day and free up plenty of your time for use at your leisure.

- How to Store and Safeguard Passwords – Simple trick will help you create and remember strong passwords.

- How to maximize your Social Security benefits – In light of the elimination of "File and Suspend" and "Restricted Application" strategies, the chart shows claiming strategies for 1) Single never married, 2) currently married, 3) married at least 10 years, divorced at least 2 years, currently single, 4) divorced, has remarried and currently married, 5) widow/widower, 6) surviving divorced spouse, married at least 10 years, currently single or remarried after the age of 60.

- Best places for retirement – Some of these retirement communities are surprising. Some viable locations have ½ the cost of living of most cities in the U.S.

- Paying for Nursing Home and Long-Term Care

- How to qualify for Medicaid benefits for LTC

- How to reduce income to qualify for Medicaid

- How to reduce assets to qualify for Medicaid.

- **Estate Planning** – How to protect your estate from estate tax and inheritance tax.

- **Enrich Your Life by Exploring the World** – Travel as soon as you can while you are still young. This chapter discusses why the money you spend traveling and exploring the world is money well spent.

- **Staying Healthy and Fit as You Age** – There are a few minor behavior modification changes that you can put into practice that will keep you healthy throughout your retirement years.

- **Live a Rich, Happy, Healthy, Simple and Balanced Life**

- **Learn more, click on the link below:**
  ****

More ABOUT THE AUTHOR

Arthur V. Prosper heads the finance department of a privately held manufacturing firm in the great state of New Jersey. Previously, he was the Vice President of Finance of the Kuoni Group and the Accounting Director of Cantel Medical. He was responsible for the financial objectives, retirement and benefit plans, investment goals and capital structures of the companies he worked for.

Supplemental Disclaimer

The use of the methods discussed in this book will likely adversely affect your credit worthiness and may result in you being subject to collections or being sued by creditors or collectors and may increase the outstanding balances of the amounts you owe prior to using the methods discussed herein. We do not guarantee that your debts will be resolved for a specific amount or percentage or within a specific period of time. Please contact a tax professional to discuss potential tax consequences of debt forgiveness.

The information contained in this book is provided to you "AS IS", for entertainment only, and does not constitute legal advice. We make no claims, promises or guarantees about the accuracy, completeness, or any specific result from the use of the contents or adequacy of the information contained in this book. Information contained in this book should not be used as substitute for obtaining legal advice from an attorney licensed or authorized to practice in your jurisdiction. The author is not a lawyer. The author and publisher and their affiliates, parents, subsidiaries, assigns, officers, directors, shareholders, employees, representatives, agents and servants assume no responsibility to any person who relies on information contained herein and disclaim all liability in respect to such information.

Copyright and Trademark Ownership

Please be aware that any unauthorized use of the contents contained herein violates copyright laws, trademark laws, the laws of privacy and publicity, and/or other regulations and statutes. All text, images and other materials provided herein are owned by **Arthur V. Prosper** unless otherwise attributed to third parties. None of the content on these materials may be copied, reproduced, distributed, downloaded, displayed, or transmitted in any form without the prior written permission of **Arthur V. Prosper**, the legal copyright owner. However, you may copy, reproduce, distribute, download, display, or transmit the content of the materials for personal, non-commercial use provided that full attribution and citation to **Arthur V. Prosper** is included and the content is not modified, and you retain all copyright and other proprietary notices contained in the content. The permission stated above is automatically rescinded if you breach any of these terms or conditions. If permission is rescinded or denied, you must immediately destroy any downloaded and/or printed content.
****

PUBLISHER: A-TEAM, LP - CATALOG:

Living Rich & Loving It: Your guide to a rich, happy, healthy, simple and balanced life Kindle Edition
https://www.amazon.com/Living-Rich-Loving-healthy-balanced-ebook/dp/B01GORIB4Y/ref=sr_1_3?s=digital-text&ie=UTF8&qid=1480539481&sr=1-3&keywords=Arthur_V._Prosper

The Simplest Path to Wealth: Turn $50,000 into $3.3 Million
https://www.amazon.com/gp/product/B01KPQB0OS/ref=dbs_a_def_rwt_bibl_vppi_i0

The Six Million Dollar Retiree: Your roadmap to a six million dollar retirement nest egg Kindle Edition
https://www.amazon.com/Six-Million-Dollar-Retiree-retirement-ebook/dp/B073XTL47J/ref=sr_1_4?s=digital-text&ie=UTF8&qid=1504026864&sr=1-4&keywords=Arthur_V._Prosper

Dynamic Budgeting Techniques: Cut your expenses in half and double your income Kindle Edition
https://www.amazon.com/Dynamic-Budgeting-Techniques-expenses-double-ebook/dp/B01LZA9O3W/ref=asap_bc?ie=UTF8

Stop Paying Your Credit Cards: Obtain Credit Card Debt Forgiveness Volume 1 Kindle Edition
https://www.amazon.com/Stop-Paying-Your-Credit-Cards-ebook/dp/B019ZY3D1E/ref=asap_bc?ie=UTF8

How Much Federal Income Tax Will I Pay in 2018?
https://www.amazon.com/Much-Federal-Income-Will-2018-ebook/dp/B078Z5LXGJ/ref=sr_1_8?s=digital-text&ie=UTF8&qid=1534698975&sr=1-8&keywords=arthur+prosper

www.ingramcontent.com/pod-product-compliance
Lightning Source LLC
Chambersburg PA
CBHW020443220526
45464CB00002B/840